THIS PROMISED LAND,
EL SALVADOR

▲▲

THIS PROMISED LAND, EL SALVADOR

▲▲▲

THE REFUGEE COMMUNITY OF COLOMONCAGUA AND THEIR RETURN TO MORAZÁN

Photographs by Steve Cagan

Text by Beth Cagan and Steve Cagan

RUTGERS UNIVERSITY PRESS ▲ NEW BRUNSWICK AND LONDON

▲▲▲

Library of Congress Cataloging-in-Publication Data

Cagan, Steve, 1943–
    This promised land, El Salvador : the refugee community of Colomoncagua and their return to
Morazán / photographs by Steve Cagan; text by Beth and Steve Cagan.
        p.   cm.
    Includes bibliographical references.
    ISBN 0-8135-1679-X
    1. Refugees—El Salvador.   2. Refugees—Honduras.   3. Refugees—El Salvador—Pictorial
works.   4. Refugees—Honduras—Pictorial works.   5. Salvadorans—Honduras.
6. Salvadorans—Honduras—Pictorial works.   7. Colomoncagua (Honduras : Refugee camp)
8. Colomoncagua (Honduras : Refugee camp)—Pictorial works.   9. Repatriation—El Salvador—
Morazán.   10. Repatriation—El Salvador—Morazán—Pictorial works.   I. Cagan, Beth,
1944–   .   II. Title.
    HV640.5.S24C34   1991
    362.87′097283′81—dc20   90-20819
                                                                                        CIP

British Cataloging-in-Publication information available.

Dr. Montes celebrating Mass in the chapel in the subcamp Copinol, August 1989.

To the memory of Dr. Segundo Montes, S.J.

FOREWORD

"SALVADORAN REFUGEES IN HONDURAS," BY DR. SEGUNDO MONTES, S.J.

▲▲

In the camp at Colomoncagua, in the community he loved and admired, he was known as "the man with the umbrella," because he was the first person whom many in the community had ever seen with an umbrella. In August of 1989, we had the good fortune to meet Dr. Montes in Colomoncagua, and spent three days with him there, often in long conversations after shared meals. He told us that the refugee community was the most extraordinary sociological experience of his life. We did not know at the time that this was to be his last visit to the community.

Dr. Montes was the head of the sociology department and the director of the Human Rights Institute at the Universidad Centroamericana, the Catholic university in San Salvador. On November 16, 1989, along with five of his Jesuit colleagues, a housekeeper, and her daughter, he was assassinated by members of the armed forces of El Salvador. Dr. Montes was one more of the too-many martyrs to the cause of peace and justice for the poor whom the people of El Salvador have had to mourn.

When the refugees from Colomoncagua returned to El Salvador to reestablish their community in northern Morazán Department, they named their settlement Ciudad Segundo Montes (Segundo Montes City) in his honor.

In the camps at Colomoncagua and San Antonio there are about ten thousand Salvadoran refugees, who fled from the violence and the war in the northeastern zone of El Salvador, on the border with Honduras. Historically, close relations have existed between the populations on both sides of the border. Before the war between the two countries—in July of 1969—the economy of the Honduran border region was very much linked to El Salvador, which provided a large market, and Salvadoran money even circu-

This article is an excerpt from Dr. Montes's book, *Refugiados y Repatriados: El Salvador y Honduras* (San Salvador: Departamento de Sociología y Ciencias Políticas, Instituto de Derechos Humanos, Universidad Centroamericana José Simeón Cañas, May 1989), 39–46. Steve Cagan translated the article into English. It was written before the refugees made their proposal to return to El Salvador.

lated as legal tender. Better communications and the proximity of more developed towns on the Salvadoran side led a great part of the Honduran population to seek health care, communications, commerce, and other goods and services in Salvadoran territory. Further, family links and connections through marriage were quite general throughout both nationalities. This facilitated the fact that upon entering Honduran territory, the Salvadoran refugee population was at first accepted, assisted, and welcomed by the Honduran population, until control and isolation were brought on in the camps.

The fact that the Salvadorans are confined in very restricted areas, isolated from the rest of the population and the country, and assisted with international aid, means that their presence and existence in Honduras represents neither a social nor an economic problem for the host country. In effect, the Salvadorans have practically no contact with the rest of the population or with Honduran society. As a result, their social interrelations would be practically nonexistent if it were not for their being held up as an example, and for the problem of political propaganda, both official and through the communications media. Nor do they represent an economic problem for Honduras, from which neither resources nor goods are directed towards their maintenance. It is rather from foreign sources that the Salvadoran refugees and the agencies—some of them domestic like Caritas—are supplied with the goods and services they need, with the exception, recently, of health care through the corresponding Honduran Ministry.

However, there is no doubt that the Salvadoran refugees in Honduras are indeed officially perceived as a high-risk political problem, being considered as family members and as a base of sympathy and support for the FMLN [the Farabundo Martí Front for National Liberation, the guerrilla organization in El Salvador]. The problem is thus inscribed in ideological and politico-military circles as a threat of infiltration and ideological/subversive contamination which might affect the neighboring population and open the possibility of problems with serious repercussions for the future of Honduras and subsequent social peace. The difference in attitude towards the Nicaraguan [refugees] can be understood in the light of this consideration; the latter do not question the society or the dominant ideology in Honduras, but rather reinforce it, even if only in their antagonism towards the governing regime in Nicaragua. Meanwhile, the Salvadoran refugees question not only the situation in their country, but the very structures of the underdeveloped and dependent countries of the region and their causes, struggling to construct a different society.

The social organization in the camps of the Salvadoran refugees is very dense and planned, with egalitarian participation of the entire population, who elect their representatives to three ascending levels, from the "colonies," or groups of dwellings and families, to the semiautonomous "sub-camps," . . . to the committees and general leadership in each of the two camps. There is a rational division of work, according to the abilities and skills of each person . . . without distinction by sex, and an assignment of work and functions for the benefit of the unit or the total community as a whole, so that all demands and needs, from production, distribution, education, health, and recreation to art, pastoral needs, security, and consciousness-raising, are all duly attended to. Nobody is abandoned, but rather nuclear social groups are formed—in the style of families—integrating widows, orphans, or other abandoned persons or invalids in quasi-familial social and psychological units. They have been able, in the end, to banish alcoholism, delinquency, drugs, idleness, and other social ills by community persuasion and by social pressure in that direction.

Both social and economic organization seem to be very much conditioned by the great ideological homogeneity which rules there, by the identification with their history and their destiny, and by the hope of returning to their country of origin when the conditions they demand—peace with justice, democracy, and liberty—exist, in order to reproduce the model they experienced in the camp and to help construct a new society to benefit the poorest people, those who for decades and centuries have been deprived of the benefits of civilization. Religion in turn constitutes another factor providing for social cohesiveness, through the shared life and the liturgical education and participation in a committed Catholicism which is professed by practically all the Salvadoran refugees. They are not divided into different confessions, but respect the tiny non-Catholic minorities, with whom there is a close collaboration and respect in the entire social life of the camps. Such a social organization cannot but generate tensions and some kind of rejection or nonacceptance in some persons. They may be pressed by the social control of the community and of the leadership, or look for different alternatives individually or in small groups, thus giving rise to external criticisms, to tensions with UNHCR [the United Nations High Commission on Refugees, which had overall responsibility for administration of the camp], or to resocialization measures and a certain internal coercion.

The economic model adopted and developed by these refugees implies a series of indispensable elements. Work is for the common benefit of the collective, and there is egalitarian reward for everyone according to their personal and/or family needs—with special attention to elderly people and malnourished children. No productive goods are held individually, nor does any money circulate, nor is it possible to acquire goods in the nonexistent internal market. Even tortillas are made in a collective way for the entire population, in order to assure this minimal food, at the same time conserving fuel, as well as work force, which can be dedicated to other productive or service areas. The diversification in work and in production is aimed at a kind of economic self-sufficiency in complementary items and sectors, optimizing the work force and the materials and equipment which are available. The economy of the Salvadorans' camp is not monetary, but isolated, closed, dependent on external aid and the provision of materials, which may generate in its members a lack of capacity for dealing with the laws of the market and competition within the external system.

The arid mountain slopes where the camps are located have been transformed into terraces to cultivate garden vegetables and fruits—there is insufficient land for the production of corn and beans, which are indispensable in their diet and therefore have to be supplied by the agencies. But at the same time, they have created and developed farm activities for the production of proteins for the community—eggs, chickens, goats for milk and meat, pigs, rabbits, ducks. Simultaneously, they have developed an industrial production of other necessary goods, in workshops and "factories" of mechanics, woodworking, shoemaking, cotton and wool clothing, sheet-metal utensils, hammock making, ceramics and crafts, sufficient for internal consumption when primary material is available. With these products they could participate in the market if they had permission and opportunities both to acquire materials and to freely sell the manufactured products. The electrical generators they have are indispensable for production, for a series of services, and even for recreation; every night as a community they watch "El Noticiero" [the news] on channel 6 of Salvadoran TV before the electricity is shut off at nine at night. As an additional demonstration of their concern for the normal development of the population and of respect for nature, of their humanism and sensitivity, they have created in Colomoncagua a little zoo so that the children might know and see nondomesticated animals.

In order to develop their economic model, not only the donation of goods and machinery, but also the supply of primary materials and other necessities have been indispensable, given the isolation to which the inhabitants of the camps are submitted. The same is true for the availability of instructors and technicians who aid in the accelerated education of each of the areas and sectors. Another indispensable factor, in addition to the organization and social structure they have adopted, is the accelerated and intensive process of self-education. Practically the entire community, children and adults, attends school—which goes from kindergarten to the sixth grade, with teachers trained in the refugee community itself—and training workshops, combining teaching with work and implanting the desire to learn because of needs which grow out of the work itself. Health is another fundamental element in the model, and it is therefore given a high priority; hygiene personnel and laboratory workers are trained to provide basic primary attention or send patients for medical care within the camp or in a hospital.

Perhaps in conditions of less confinement, with a laxer social organization, with less homogeneity of ideas and objectives, without help and assistance for nourishment and production, or without good instructors, it might not have been possible to accomplish the success of this model. However, neither can it be accomplished by the previous conditions alone, for there has to exist a human group with those characteristics of work, spirit, community selflessness, and hope.

The profound change effectuated in that population during their stay in the camps is a phenomenon possibly unique, and worthy of study, analysis, and learning for its guidelines and values. Before, it was a community with individualistic structures and behavior, more than 85 percent illiterate, which used the most primitive techniques—practically pre-Columbian—to cultivate the land in extremely poor parcels, left behind by the advances of civilization and isolated from the processes of the society in general. In a few years—the process of organization and training for production began in 1983—they have converted themselves into a population with a high degree of solidarity, more than 85 percent literate, which utilizes new methods and techniques of cultivation; manages animal farming with good feeding and sanitary techniques; runs complicated mechanical and electrical equipment; plans, keeps books, and audits in production, distribution, and inventory; trains it own educators and sanitary workers, its leaders, and all the personnel needed to keep the model going ahead; perfects itself, diversifies, and complements itself. The necessary levels of leadership, of training, of intellectual and manual development, of capacity for abstraction and synthesis, on the one hand seem impossible to reach in such a short time. On the other hand, they serve to undo a series of myths about the peasant population: their mythic and traditional fatalism, their atavistic worldview, their superstitious attitude rooted in the past. They demonstrate their capacity for change, for analytic reflection, for accelerated adaptation and empowerment, for organization, leadership, social and enterprise management. At the same time, they open the possibility that a society configured by such elements could indeed be possible—and to the extent that they can be extended and applied to Salvadoran society in general, might convert El Salvador from a country which because of different indicators and perspectives is frequently considered not viable, into one which is.

The relations of the refugee Salvadorans in the camps we visited towards institutions and the surrounding population are of a different nature. With the officials of UNHCR there is a tense relationship of insisting, demands, diverse pressures, at the same time that they value their indispensable protection and assistance and currently want them to sleep in the very camp as a security guarantee for the refugees. While it is true that the officials of UNHCR feel that demands beyond their mandate are sometimes put on them and that there is tension in their relations with the Salvadoran refugees, on the other hand they perceive that their work is made very good use of by the latter and that their dynamism and even their demanding is for a greater and better development of the community. With the volunteers of the other agencies, there is a more positive relationship, given the cover which they provide, the generous sharing of life, the great training service, the option for and identification with the refugees—it is necessary to exclude the relationship with Doctors Without Borders [Médecins Sans Frontières, or MSF], who were expelled from the camp by a decision of the Salvadoran refugees after a series of problems and tensions which it is not appropriate to evaluate here.

With respect to the surrounding Honduran population, we have already indicated the traditional ties which unite them, and the support which they received in the beginning. Currently, the relationship between the two populations is minimal or practically nonexistent, not only because of the isolation of the camps, but also because of the pressure of the Honduran civilian and military authorities to impede relationships and the possible ideological-political contamination of the population of the zone. The Honduran communities get no more benefit than some sporadic services which are also extended to them in cases of emergency, or some insignificant economic benefits derived from the presence of the agencies. They find themselves faced with anxiety about their comparative disadvantage, whether in the supply of goods and services (water and electricity are not the least of these, although UNHCR has helped in some projects of this kind for that community) or in the existence of the model of education, training, organization, technical advance, and development in the camps. The population in the camp is similar to theirs in origin, and linked by strong ties of family, commercial, and social relationships, but is nonetheless inaccessible to them. The Honduran population surrounding the camps of the Salvadoran refugees sees itself impeded and denied the right to take advantage of an opportunity, possibly unique in their lives, to learn and receive training for a new kind of life and society, because of the danger of ideological-political contamination. This is not only an incomprehensible frustration for them, but a waste of human and material resources in an unrepeatable moment, against their interest, their communities, and the entirety of Honduran society. The backwardness in technical areas and in levels of life of the surrounding rural Honduran population can be perceived, among other indicators, by the fact that they admire the sight of little villages lighted up in the night in Salvadoran territory, something which is unfamiliar to them, removed from their realizable aspirations, and spectacular.

CONTENTS

▲▲

LIST OF MAPS AND FIGURES

▲▲

ACKNOWLEDGMENTS

▲▲

The authors wish to acknowledge with gratitude the following people for their help in making this book possible:

First, the community in Colomoncagua and Meanguera and our many new friends there, too numerous to mention individually, for their encouragement of the project, and for their openness, hospitality, and warmth. We also must thank them for sharing documents from their carefully maintained archive.

Numerous current and former staff members of the humanitarian agencies and UNHCR—Hondurans, Europeans, and North Americans—who helped us with information and background.

Laura Jackson, of radio station WHYY-FM, Philadelphia, who shared transcripts of interviews with refugees.

Barbara Wein and the staff of Voices on the Border for their support in this project, and for their work on behalf of the community.

Numerous friends for their encouragement, especially Stu Greenberg for his assistance in allowing our computers to talk to each other, and Jim Miller, Deborah Van Kleef, Claudia Reiter, Kathleen Greenberg, and Jessie Cagan for their criticisms and suggestions about the text and photographs, and to all of them for various kinds of help extended in moments when it was needed and appreciated.

The staff at Rutgers University Press, especially Marlie Wasserman, Ken Arnold, Barbara Kopel, Steve Maikowski, and Kate Harrie, who so readily understood what we were trying to accomplish with this book and helped so much in making that a reality. Our agent, Edy Selman, for her support and work on our behalf.

Finally, our daughters, Joanna and Shauna, for their enthusiasm, support, and courage, and for their love and patience.

The research for this book was made possible in part by funds provided by Cleveland State University and Rutgers University.

All the quotations in this book, unless otherwise indicated, are from the refugees themselves—from interviews or from documents they produced. In some places, we have changed people's names in order to protect their identity.

THIS PROMISED LAND, EL SALVADOR

▲▲▲

We believe that we have lived in our own flesh the same circumstances that the people of Israel experienced in their Exodus, walking through foreign lands, suffering and crying out, but always having the help of God, and with very firm hope and faith. This same Liberating God is giving us a promised land, that we know by the name of El Salvador.

Christian Base Community of the
refugees at Colomoncagua, Honduras

I thought that there was no future for El Salvador, but upon seeing your model of organization and development, I changed my mind.

Dr. Segundo Montes, S.J.

This book is about refugees from El Salvador who left their country fleeing government bombs and repression and the ravages of a bloody civil war. It is the story of over eight thousand Salvadorans who lived for almost a decade in a refugee camp in Colomoncagua, Honduras. In the midst of the hardships of exile, these people became a community, and as a community they returned to their homeland to build a new life. Theirs is a story that begins with tragedy and suffering, but ends in triumph and hope.

INTRODUCTION

▲▲▲▲▲▲▲▲▲▲▲▲▲▲▲▲▲▲▲▲▲▲

INTRODUCTION

▲▲▲

One afternoon in August of 1989, we arrived in the village of Colomoncagua, near the Salvadoran border, in the mountainous Honduran department
of Intibucá. We had spent the day traveling from the capital, Tegucigalpa,
by the method most people, Hondurans or foreigners, use for the trip: first
an early morning bus out the highway to the northwest to the town of Sigua-
tepeque, where the route leaves paved roads; then in another bus over a nar-
row but dramatic sierra filled with coffee and banana, down and across the
fertile valley of Otoro, the fields lush and green at that time of year, followed
by a much higher climb into a greater mountain range in whose heights lies
the departmental capital of La Esperanza. There we found a ride on one of
the battered pickup trucks that carry passengers and cargo on the winding
roads that follow the gradual downward slope of the mountains south to the
border with El Salvador.

Late in the afternoon, we approached the village of Colomoncagua. Although we had descended some distance from La Esperanza, we were still in
rugged and beautiful mountains, a zone that seemed harsh to us, with reddish soil and sparse vegetation, except for the scraggly pines. Black buz-
zards, called *zopilotes* here, flew lazily about, bold as crows back home.
Like much of Honduras, the area was sparsely populated, but an occasional
little stucco house with a tile roof could be seen from the deeply gutted dirt
road. Now we were very close to the Salvadoran border. From the road leading to the village, much of eastern El Salvador is visible; the volcanos of
San Miguel and San Vicente are prominent features of the landscape.

Finally, we found ourselves on the cobblestoned streets of the village. Although it is one of the major centers of that corner of Honduras, Colomoncagua is essentially a sleepy town of several hundred people, which has

*Overleaf: From the road to the village of Colomoncagua, looking to the south. In
the distance the mountains of El Salvador can be seen.*

A classic peasant house of the area. Note the abundance of plants, including bananas and other fruits.

attracted more than its share of international attention because of the nearby camp for refugees from El Salvador.

We had come to this remote area to visit the camp, also called Colomoncagua, home to some eighty-four hundred Salvadorans who had fled the bombings and repression in their country and had been in this place for as long as nine years. Steve had been asked to go to the camp as a photographer in early 1988, to help launch a campaign in the United States in support of the refugee community. It was his third trip in a year and a half (and his fourth since 1982). In his previous visits, photographing, interviewing, and collecting materials for the campaign, he had come to admire, respect, and love the people there. For Beth, who had been working in the same campaign in Cleveland, it was the first visit.

Like many who knew about the refugee camp at Colomoncagua, we had been impressed by the apparently extraordinary achievements of the people

A view of the subcamp Limón II, with terraced gardens in the foreground.

there. Now we had come to study more formally the social and organizational structures the refugees had created, to get a more accurate sense of daily life in the camp, and to understand better how they were able to accomplish so much and in what ways they might serve as a model for other poor people in the region. These questions had taken on some urgency as the refugees had recently announced their intention to return to El Salvador and reestablish their form of community in northern Morazán Department.

Having arrived in the town, we had to follow a series of steps in order to enter the camp. In Tegucigalpa we had secured permission to visit the camp from the Comisión Nacional para Refugiados (CONARE), the Honduran government agency charged with overseeing the refugee situation. Now we made a courtesy call at the United Nations High Commission for Refugees (UNHCR) field office in the town, and then went to the government immigration delegation and the local military commander to have our permissions signed and stamped. Finally, grimy and weary from the journey, but happy to have all our documents in order and eager to get to the camp, we left the military office to look for a ride with whoever might be driving up there.

At that moment, we heard a series of distant, but distinct, explosions. One, two, three . . . in all, a dozen: 500-pound bombs being dropped by small planes over the border in El Salvador's Morazán Department, the very area to which the refugees were planning to return. It was an unsettling moment. Suddenly, the war in El Salvador seemed very close. And, we wondered, how could they be planning to return to *that,* the very bombing and repression that had driven them out in the first place? It was a question we were to come back to many times while we were there.

For the next two weeks we lived in the camp, sharing the home of a refugee family and becoming part of the community for that brief time. We mingled and wandered freely about through all of the nine subcamps that made up Colomoncagua, taking pictures and making sound recordings, interviewing scores of people (refugees and international agency workers alike), sitting in on meetings, gathering numerous documents prepared by the refugees, and observing and participating in daily life in the camp. People responded to us with a combination of curiosity, shyness, and warmth. They were accustomed to visitors, especially foreigners, but when they learned that we would be there for a full two weeks they beamed with pleasure, as most stayed only for a few days. By the end of the two weeks we had become close friends with some and felt like comfortable neighbors with many more. At our *despedida,* the farewell ceremony the refugees held for all visitors, there were some tears and many embraces and warm handshakes. "We'll see you next year in El Salvador," we pledged, although we were not certain this would be possible—for them or us. As it turned out, it was.

Portrait made in the camp at Colomoncagua.

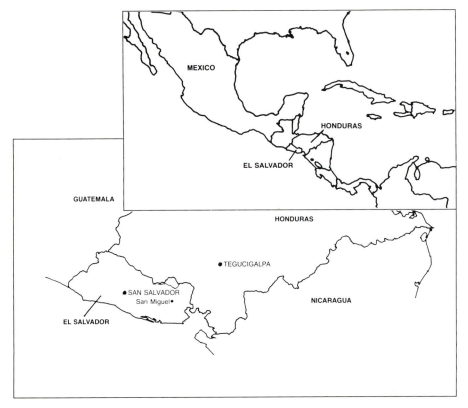

Locating El Salvador in the region

Steve was able to return to Colomoncagua for a month-long stay in January of 1990, when the community was in the process of returning to their country. He was one of the first internationals allowed by the Salvadoran authorities to cross the border with the refugees, and spent a day in the new resettlement in northern Morazán Department, sharing their excitement about finally being home. In March, he was present at the dedication ceremonies for the new city they were constructing in Meanguera, Morazán. Both of us spent time there during June and July of 1990, gathering materials for our final chapter.

This book is based on the experiences of this remarkable group of people, learned through our conversations with them and with those who assisted them. This is their story.

▲   ▲   ▲

Any but the most callous reader of the history of El Salvador will come away with a sharp sense of the long suffering of the Salvadoran poor. Uprooted from the land, first by European conquerors and then by an oligarchy bent on extending its privileges through alliances with the military, Sal-

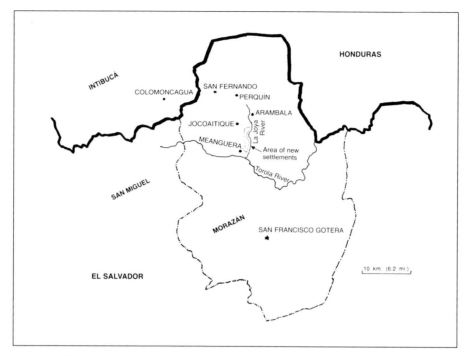

Morazán Department

vadoran *campesinos* (peasants) have struggled to eke out a living from the
little land and work available to them. Despite literally centuries of repressive rule, they have persisted in trying to better their lives, building
unions and cooperatives, setting up peasant organizations, pastoral groups,
and other grassroots organizations to defend their interests—and have paid
for these efforts in countless murders, disappearances, beatings, and threats.

By the late 1970s, this general climate of repression and terror had escalated into a full-blown civil war when opposition groups realized the impos-
sibility of peaceful change and took up arms. Emboldened and reinforced by
huge amounts of military aid from the United States, the Salvadoran regime
attempted to eliminate all opponents of its rule. By some estimates, one-
quarter of the population of this tiny country of five and a half million people
have become refugees or displaced persons since 1980.

The camp at Colomoncagua was one of several set up on the Salvadoran-
Honduran border to accommodate the victims of this cruel civil war. Beginning in December of 1980, thousands of refugees sought protection there.
By the mid-1980s the population in this UNHCR-administered camp had
reached almost 8,400, mostly campesinos from nearby Morazán, a department (i.e., state or province) in northeastern El Salvador, one of the poorest
in the country.

They came to Colomoncagua frightened and miserable, all touched intimately by violence and destruction. The Honduran government reacted
to their presence with distrust, viewing them as guerrillas; a military en-

Portrait made in the camp at Colomoncagua.

Two boys take refuge from a tropical storm in a workshop in the camp.

circlement was set up around the camp to prevent "contamination" of the neighboring Honduran population. For almost a decade, the refugees were confined to the camp; they called it "the prison without walls." They longed to return home and to be free.

At the same time, however, the camp had a much more positive meaning for the refugees. Assisted by dedicated staff from humanitarian agencies under contract with the UNHCR, primarily Caritas, an international Catholic relief organization; the U.S.-based Catholic Relief Services and Mennonite Central Committee; and CEDEN, a Protestant Honduran relief agency, the refugees transformed themselves from illiterate, untutored peasants into a skilled, sophisticated, and cohesive community. Colomoncagua was a school for them.

The accomplishments of the community during their nine years of exile are impressive. They protected themselves against raids by Honduran soldiers and cutbacks in assistance by the UNHCR, and managed to resist attempts to relocate the camp far away from the border. They developed a well-functioning and democratic internal government, establishing a communal life-style in which all had equal rights to resources and no one lived better than anyone else. They conducted cultural and educational programs for adults and children, ending illiteracy and developing a cadre of trained teachers, and they promoted improved awareness of health, sanita-

Friendship is expressed during a tranquil moment in the chapel in Limones.

C H A P T E R ▲ O N E

EXODUS

THE FLIGHT FROM EL SALVADOR

▲▲

> The thousand gullies we had to cross at night when there was nothing to eat—you don't forget that.

It seems that there is a story of horror for every village and hamlet in the northeastern departments of Morazán, San Miguel, and La Unión, the regions in El Salvador from which most of the refugees at Colomoncagua had fled. They left their towns—Mozote, Perquín, La Guacamaya, Joateca, Cerro Pando, San Fernando—not just because of war, but because of a particularly cruel civil conflict in which their government considered them the enemy because of their call for a more just society. Free-fire zones, scorched-earth campaigns, pacification programs—techniques perfected by the United States military in Viet-Nam and taught to their Salvadoran allies—meant that civilians, especially in the countryside, were fair game.

It is only terrible fear and suffering that forces people to leave their homes and farms, that uproots them from their communities, that tears them from their former lives. For the refugees of Colomoncagua, these experiences were the common tragedy that had forced them into exile and the source of the remarkable unity that developed in the camp: "We came here because of the repression, the bombings. The thousand gullies we had to cross at night when there was nothing to eat, you don't forget that. And when we go back, we won't forget that."

Rufina Amaya is one of the few survivors of the infamous massacre at Mozote, in which almost one thousand people were mercilessly slaughtered in November of 1981 by the notorious U.S.-trained Atlacatl Battalion of the Salvadoran armed forces—ironically, the same battalion responsible for murdering the Jesuit priests eight years later. She describes her experiences on that fateful day:

Overleaf: Rooftops in Limón I. The banner reads, We Want to Repatriate Voluntarily, Not with Pressure from Cutbacks in Assistance.

CHAPTER

1

▲▲▲▲▲▲▲▲▲▲▲▲▲▲▲▲▲▲▲▲▲

tion, and nutrition. They ran a technical training school, an auto mechanics workshop, and many training and production workshops, producing almost all the goods used in the camp. They wrote and produced their own weekly newspaper and other publications and documents, including three periodicals directed toward the international community. They coordinated and hosted numerous visits to the camp by foreign observers—journalists, diplomats, researchers, religious delegations—maintaining correspondence with groups all over the world, effectively advocating for their own collective interests on the local, national, and international level. They negotiated with officials from the Salvadoran and Honduran governments, winning a set of conditions that permitted their repatriation as a community, and then planned and administered the move and the construction of the new settlement in Meanguera, Morazán.

The refugees saw themselves as like the ancient Hebrews in the desert, who had created a new, self-reliant and mutually supportive community and then decided it was time to cross the river and return to their promised land.

Most of all, they thrust themselves forward into a future that they had constructed, a product of the new consciousness they had carved out of their extraordinary circumstances and experiences. They began as refugees, frightened and helpless, and they ended as citizens of a new land.

> Maybe it was the helicopter that brought the order to kill all the people, because after [it landed] they began to tie the hands of all the men and to blindfold them. And they threw them face down on the ground, on top of one another, and they stood on top of them. . . . And then they entered to where [the women and children] were, with knives in their hands and with their guns. They went close to the children and the children began to scream, and the mothers too. And then about ten o'clock I could see that they were killing the men, they were cutting off their heads and throwing them into the convent. I had my baby at my breast when I saw that they were killing the men, and I said to the other women, "They're going to kill us." And then women screamed and prayed—no one could stand the terrible things that were happening to the people.

Managing somehow to escape in the midst of this frenzy of death, and forced to leave her four children behind, Rufina watched from her hiding place as they torched the town and murdered its entire population.

> I was there when I heard that they were killing the children. You could hear the cries of the children, calling out for their mothers, crying out that they were being killed, that they were having their throats slit with the knives. And you didn't hear any gunshots. They were hanging them. You didn't hear any shots, only the cries of the children that they were being killed, the bigger children and the little ones, the great crying that you could hear. At that moment I prayed to the Lord that he give me strength not to go back, because I wanted to go back and throw myself in the street because I heard the screams of my children.

After several days of furtive escape, Rufina linked up with other refugees fleeing from similar atrocities, who were making their way across the border to Colomoncagua, arriving at the camp in a group of four hundred. The flight took a few days for some, up to two weeks for others. The refugees walked mainly at night, in fear of attacks by helicopters, hiding in caves and surviving on water, bananas, sugarcane, and whatever bits of food they were able to find. Two children were born along the way, and many died.

When interviewed in the camp by North American visitors nine years later, Rufina admitted it was painful to relive her experiences. "But when I was there, hidden, I always asked God that if I would survive, it would be to tell the story, because this is a story of life and of suffering in the war in my country. We were defenseless because we didn't know what a war was, we didn't know anything. We just lived there, farming. So many people who didn't know anything and to have to suffer this terrible massacre—it's a great injustice against all of us."

Above and opposite: A mother and daughter in the nutrition center of Quebrachito.

Most of the refugees who sought asylum in Colomoncagua were victims of similar attacks on the many villages and towns in Morazán Department, many of them as vicious as the massacre at Mozote though less well-known. The experiences of Ignacia M., from the *cantón* (township) Delicias de Concepción, are typical: "The army killed two of my sons and my mother-in-law in the cottage where she lived. They burnt her with all her possessions. She was an elderly woman, seventy-five years old. We only managed to bury the bones that had not burned. We fled with very undernourished children. We didn't have anything to eat, as the soldiers had robbed us of everything. When they told us there was a refuge, we set out in the rain. On the way we met other people, and that's how we arrived at this refuge."

Doña Paquita recalls details of her flight: "You should have seen us in '80, running through the countryside. I was with five children—we slept by the side of a river. We ran here and there to avoid death. . . . We slept

one night in a *quebrada* (ravine), and twelve soldiers so very close. . . .
With a rag I covered the mouth of the little one so she wouldn't cry out.
That's how we would pass the night, and early in the morning we would
leave again."

María R. fled from Los Quebrachos, another tiny village in Morazán.

> There was a lot of repression there. The military was bombing us,
> what they call "scorched earth," where nothing was left. They
> did that, but we left our homes and were in the mountains because
> we saw that they had already killed a lot of people and we
> couldn't do anything there. We were women, and so we fled with
> the children to the mountains [where they stayed for three
> months]. . . . We had suffered a great deal in El Salvador. They
> had killed so many of our families, that's why we were looking

During a Sunday mass.

for help. It was very hard. Some couldn't leave because they were sick. They were defenseless; they didn't understand. . . . They were burned in their own homes. But we looked for refuge and they gave us protection here.

We got here in December of 1980. First the Hondurans gave us help. People came from the little villages around and gave us food. But we were still about three days here in the town before we got food. And then the church came and gave us help, Father Correa and another priest. And so in this way they brought us little things, others bananas or bread or flour. It was a flour we didn't know, and we made *atol* [a sweet drink, usually made from corn] without sugar in the evening and gave it to the smallest children. Many children got sick and had terrible diarrhea, since they hadn't eaten in so long. The old people got sick, too. We were better off, being younger and stronger. We got sick but it wasn't so bad. Then we were transferred here to the camps.

When the refugees first arrived in Honduras, desperate and helpless, they believed they would stay for a week or two and then return home. None of them knew that they would remain in their new setting for almost ten long years. The first group, six hundred of them, arrived on Honduran soil on December 13, 1980. The next day, another group of four hundred arrived, entering through the village of Las Flores. They were met by representatives of the United Nations and the Catholic church, through Caritas. "We arrived

In a guardería.

at Colomoncagua," the refugees later wrote in a document they produced about their history, "where a part of the group stayed while the other was taken to the airfield. Some lived for several days in the church, others in the market, not only suffering from the very cold weather of that time, but also from threats from the Honduran armed forces."

According to UNHCR, there was some resentment in the town because the refugees were receiving aid from the United Nations, while the residents of the area, themselves terribly poor, were not offered assistance. The refugees thought it was rather the Honduran military presence that prevented a friendlier response from local residents, because at first they were treated with sympathy by many Hondurans in the surrounding area. One woman described her experience: "The first few days I lived on the porch of a house. The lady gave me food. On the third day, she told me that she was very sorry, she had nothing against me, but she couldn't give me any more food. The military had told her not to, and she was afraid."

At first, the refugees lived in the town of Colomoncagua, seeking whatever shelter they could find and whatever assistance was offered to them. Soon, however, tensions caused them to be moved to a site about five kilometers away, where a camp was being built. There they had to live in canvas tents—"with all the difficulties with hygiene, and so forth," as they later wrote,—until more permanent structures could be completed. "It was difficult to carry out daily life, and this is why we began to organize ourselves collectively. The collective kitchen was one of our first accomplishments, where tortillas are made for the entire population."

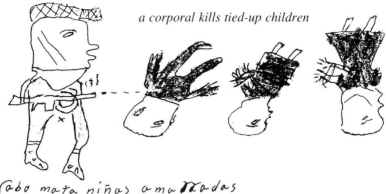

a corporal kills tied-up children

Cabo mata niñas amarradas

hung, being dragged

orcada arrastrandola

DaWizion mata monditas

a soldier, Davidson, kills nuns

Children's Drawings of the Repression in Morazán

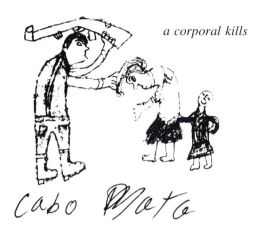

a corporal kills

Cabo Mata

killing

matando

muere orcado
enel arbol

he dies, hung from a tree

guardias

national guard

A meeting of the Congregation of Christian Men for Peace.

María R. describes the experiences of that first group who arrived in Colomoncagua in December of 1980:

> It wasn't easy. No one wanted to just donate land for us to use. The military were there. One time there was a meeting in the town, and a woman told me to go and see what they were saying, that they were talking about the refugees. And I went there, and a military man asked what I was doing there, had I been invited? And I said, "Yes, I was invited." And he said, "Get out of here before I give you a swift kick." So I left, but I had heard what they were saying. There were agencies that wanted to help us and people who were in solidarity with us, and they stayed talking about where they were going to put us. Later they agreed on this place, which is called Callejones. They had to negotiate with the owner of this place. And after a few days he began to be hassled for having let us use this land. But these lands have been paid for. The government of Honduras didn't donate these lands, nor anyone else here. This was bought with humanitarian assistance from other countries. But they took away the owner of this land to Marcala [a military base]. He said it was only being rented and finally they let him go.

Having fled from inconceivable brutality and violence in their own country, the refugees found themselves unwelcome guests in a nearby land, tolerated but distrusted; assisted, but only under extreme conditions of confinement, isolation, and harassment. These difficult conditions were the backdrop to the refugees' attempts to build a new life, forcing them into a high degree of unity and militance. Their faith and spirit had been tested first by the horrors that caused their exodus, and were challenged further by the hardships they faced in the land of their exile.

LIFE IN EXILE

▲▲▲

*We are sent like sheep in the midst of wolves, but even so we trust
that the Living Presence has accompanied us during exile.*

By early 1981, there were more than thirty thousand Salvadoran refugees in
various camps in Honduras. The official response of the Honduran government was to deny them refugee status and try to keep them near the border,
hoping they would soon return to El Salvador. On the one hand, there had
been a history of conflict in the border region between the two countries,
where land-hungry peasants from El Salvador had spilled over into under-
populated Honduras, culminating in the short-lived but nasty "Soccer War"
of 1969. The fighting was ended by a treaty arranged by the Organization of
American States, but tensions remained strong. The exact location of the
border in that area remains under dispute.

On the other hand, the traditional links—through marriage, friendship,
economic relationships—between the peasants on both sides of the border
meant to Honduran authorities that the Salvadorans, with their presumed ties
to revolutionary movements in El Salvador, represented a threat to Honduran
political stability.

The Salvadoran and Honduran governments and military establishments
thus found themselves in a temporary and sometimes rough alliance. They
certainly identified a common enemy in the FMLN (Farabundo Martí Front
for National Liberation) of El Salvador. A 1980 treaty stipulated that Salvadoran guerrillas be kept from the border region, and throughout the 1980s
Honduran military units would cross over the border to engage the guerrillas, harass Salvadoran villagers, and occasionally participate in joint military activities with the Salvadoran army.

In January 1981, the refugee commission set up by the Honduran government met with private voluntary agencies and agreed that Honduras would
respect the right of *non-refoulement*, the principle established under the Geneva convention that refugees would not be sent back if they faced political
persecution. But the Honduran government would not let the refugees work
and confined them to designated border zones in camps controlled by the

Overleaf: Saying the Lord's Prayer during Mass, Copinol.

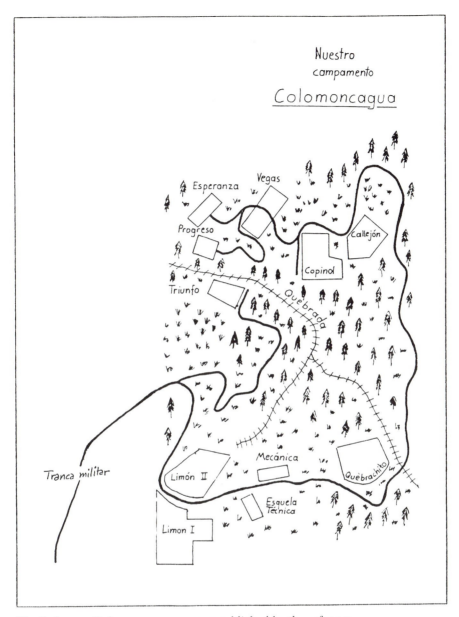

The Refuge at Colomoncagua, a map published by the refugees

military. There were two such camps established in this border area: one at San Antonio, with about twelve hundred refugees, and Colomoncagua, with more than eighty-four hundred by the late 1980s.

The camp at Colomoncagua, just a few kilometers from the border with El Salvador, was made up of nine subcamps arranged along a circular dirt road about five miles in length, nestled in the slopes of the mountains around a large, deep quebrada. Some of the subcamps were right next to each other, and some were a half-hour's strenuous walk apart. The refuge was divided

The subcamp Limón II.

into two zones, an upper and a lower, essentially on either side of the quebrada and connected by the road.

Most of the vegetation was thin, tall pine trees, and many of these had been cut down when the subcamps were constructed, leaving the buildings very exposed to the weather. The soil was quite infertile: in the rainy season the reddish earth became slippery mud; in the dry season it would turn to dust.

The buildings in the camp were mostly roughly made long wooden structures (the tents were replaced in 1983) with galvanized, corrugated metal roofs. These roofs, which have become very common in the region, replacing tile and thatch, are hot in the sun and noisy in the rain, which at the height of the rainy season is daily and intense.

Each subcamp had a small open area, a little plaza where the Social Communications program would have an office and a bulletin board with news, signs, and messages. This was the subcamp's information center and post office, and a place for people to gather. Social Communications worked on ways to keep the community informed. By the mid-1980s, they were monitoring radio news and distributing mimeographed bulletins. These were replaced in 1989 by a daily news report given over public address systems in each subcamp, prepared by excerpting news items—without editorial comment—from commercial radio stations in San Salvador, Voice of America, Voice of Nicaragua, and Radio Venceremos (a radio station of the FMLN).

The community was also kept in touch with the larger world through television. During the late 1980s, a television set—a gift from the international agencies—was placed in a public location in each subcamp with electricity (all but three) so that the people could watch commercial Salvadoran sta-

The alley between viviendas, subcamp El Copinol.

In the subcamp Callejón.

tions a few hours each day. The adults preferred news shows and *telenovelas* ("soaps"), while children liked cartoons and comedy shows.

Most of the other buildings were *viviendas* (dwellings). These were actually longhouses divided into tiny household units (after nine years, still commonly called *carpas,* or tents), which were partitioned into two or more rooms. Family units were separated from each other by thin boards, so that conversations and the cries of babies could easily be heard from one to the other. Many viviendas lacked windows, but all had two doors, which during the day were kept open to admit light and air and at night were shut against the rain or cold and to keep out the cows. Free-ranging beasts owned by Hondurans, the cows wandered about in the camp, sometimes damaging gardens or injuring people.

Each vivienda had a tiny cooking area, usually attached outside of the rest of the house to keep the smoke out. The viviendas had no electricity or running water, although most subcamps had lights in some of the public buildings and a faucet for water. Casual washing was done from barrels, captured rain or stream water, or a community *pila* (sink). Serious bathing and

Overleaf: Washing clothing in the quebrada.

Lining up to fill water containers. The water system serving the few faucets scattered through the camp was chlorinated, which the refugees did not like even though they recognized the hygiene benefits.

laundering was done in the quebrada, in wells that had been put into the creek, surrounded by trees and brush, that separated the upper and lower zones.

There were schools and workshops and warehouses there too, and chapels and nutrition centers and health stations, but from the outside the buildings were hard for visitors to distinguish. They varied in size and shape, but were all built from similar materials, except for an occasional older structure with clay brick walls. The buildings were jammed together, with little alleyways in between. Walking through these alleys, it was possible to see into everyone's living space, making personal life quite public and reinforcing the sense of shared lives.

Each cluster of viviendas had a set of latrines nearby, usually set up higher on the hillside. Most of these contained six or more cement seats with walls that didn't reach all the way to the roof, for ventilation. There were no separate latrines for men and women, and people were modest but unperturbed by these arrangements. The smell was strong and the flies bothersome, but the latrines were cleaned daily. Indeed, one of the first impressions that a visitor had was that the subcamp was not a slum, but rather an extremely clean, although very poor, settlement.

The reddish brown of the slopes surrounding the camps contrasted sharply with the green of the terraced irrigated gardens the refugees planted to supplement their limited diet, provided by UNHCR, of corn tortillas, rice, and beans. Agency vehicles—typically sturdy four-wheel-drive Toyota jeeps overflowing with refugees hitching a ride to one subcamp or another—which belonged to the UN and the other five humanitarian organizations that serviced the camps, would buzz along the rough roads inside the camp.

To a foreign visitor, Colomoncagua was a terribly impoverished place, an odd blend of a poor, semi-urban neighborhood set in the midst of rural barrenness. To enter the camp, one had to pass through a *tranca,* a Honduran military checkpoint with a rough gate across the road, where armed teenage soldiers examined one's papers and searched one's belongings—adding to the harsh atmosphere of the place.

From the beginning, the Honduran government approached the refugees with distrust and hostility, seeing them as guerrilla collaborators who used Colomoncagua as a sanctuary for FMLN combatants and a source of supplies and fresh recruits. The camp was under surveillance by the Honduran armed forces, and none of the refugees was allowed to leave except under unusual circumstances such as medical emergencies. Inside, the refugees were essentially prisoners, subject to harassment and intimidation by the Honduran soldiers. In nine years of the camp's existence, the toll of repression was heavy: forty-six refugees were killed, thirty-four disappeared, eleven were deported, three were raped, and many more were beaten or captured.

▲   ▲   ▲

Doña Nacha is an elderly, heavy-set woman. She and her husband had lost children in El Salvador and fled to Colomoncagua in 1980 with the surviving family members. Sitting in her dwelling, with great-nephews and nieces running around and roosters creating a racket inside the house, she explained what happened to her father:

> In 1981, Honduran soldiers came to the tent. They asked for my father and a couple of younger men by name. They weren't here then; they were working in a garden. That night, I asked my father to stay away from the tent, because I thought they would come back. But he said he didn't want to hide.
>
> The next day, the soldiers came back. They took my father and two young men away. He was eighty-one years old. Then we heard that they had handed all three of them over to Salvadoran soldiers in the village, who took them back to El Salvador. We never heard anything more about them. I'm sure they killed them there.

Doña Nacha's story was not unique, especially in the early years of the community's exile. Another refugee explained:

> Since we have been staying here, they [Honduran soldiers] have bothered us day and night. First, in 1982 they came into the camps to search [and] said we had enough food for three or four months, and so they stopped our food supply from coming in for some time in 1982. . . . There wasn't anything to give the children to eat; all that we had was used up. From then on the soldiers

began to search the camps regularly, . . . day and night. We were
always on the lookout for them to see what they were going to do.
We confronted them and yelled that we didn't want the military
here because we were fleeing from the military in El Salvador.
But they kept coming.

Sometimes these raids were deadly. "I was standing near the mill," re-
ported one woman, "when [the soldiers] said to me to bring out my husband
who [they claimed] was a guerrilla. I told them to get him themselves, to
open the door themselves. And they opened fire on the house; eighty-five
shots were fired. I was hit in the back by one of them. So I fell wounded by a
tree there. The next day, when we opened the door to the mill, we found the
big sacks of corn completely shot up. We didn't eat that corn. They carried
off one of the people that they killed here. We didn't know where they carried him to, but we never saw him again."

Protecting themselves from Honduran soldiers was one persistent challenge for the community. Another and greater threat was the attempt by the
Honduran government to relocate them away from the border. Beginning in
December 1983, the refugees were given three choices: repatriate to El Salvador, relocate to a third country, or be moved to a new camp to be built at
Olanchito, about 350 miles inland, where they would be joined by refugees
from two other camps.

The refugees strenuously rejected the plan, aware of what had happened
to similar refugee communities at La Virtud and Guarita, which in 1981–
1982 were relocated away from the border to Mesa Grande, where promises
of better conditions were found to have been misleading. The refugees ar-
gued that their hard-won gains in developing a suitable physical and social
infrastructure in Colomoncagua would be undermined by relocation. And
being so far from the border would make it impossible for refugees from the
continued violence in El Salvador to find their way to the camp. Moreover,
they knew that the Honduran government wanted to use the camp area at
Colomoncagua for a military base, taking advantage of its vast view of
northeastern El Salvador. This would serve only to prolong the war and
strengthen the hand of the Salvadoran military, which worked closely with
the Honduran armed forces.

The refugees were to conduct a six-year campaign against forced relocation or repatriation, insisting on their right to stay at Colomoncagua until
conditions in El Salvador made it possible for them to return there. The campaign included mass rallies and demonstrations inside the camp, publication
of numerous statements to the international community, and much public
agitation. In the end, they were successful, but at a significant cost.

In January 1984, Colonel Abraham Turcios, the head of CONARE, the
Honduran government agency responsible for refugee affairs, announced to
the refugees that Colomoncagua was needed for a military base. If they re-
fused to leave, he told them, machine guns would "turn you all to dust" and
the camp would be evacuated with tear-gas bombs and burned to the ground,
no matter what the cost in bloodshed. By 1985 a military cordon was set up

around the camp; all those entering or leaving were searched at a military checkpoint. Surveillance by helicopter and by soldiers with fixed bayonets patrolling inside the camp became routine. Patrols were as frequent as three a day and sometimes involved Salvadoran soldiers as well as Honduran. On one occasion, a Caritas staff member accused of sympathizing with the guerrillas was detained for three days and beaten by the Honduran army.

The repression and intimidation reached a climax in August 1985, when two hundred Honduran troops entered the subcamp of Callejón, claiming to be searching for guerrillas supposedly hiding there. Soldiers opened fire in all directions, dragging people out of their houses by their hair, beating and stabbing them with bayonets. Three refugees were killed, among them a two-month-old infant, who was kicked to death by a soldier, and a seventy-year-old deaf mute. More than fifty others were injured in the attack, including sixteen women who were severely beaten and two four-year-olds wounded by bullets. Relief workers tried to intervene but were trampled by the troops. Ten refugees were captured, even though they all had official identity cards confirming their refugee status. (They were eventually granted asylum in Canada.) UNHCR issued a formal protest against the raids, as did the Roman Catholic bishop for that region of Honduras and the archdiocese of San Salvador. This brutal incident left a mark on the consciousness of the refugees, and a crude memorial shelter was erected over the graves of the victims.

Colonel Turcios returned to the camp in late 1987, unannounced and unidentified, in a private vehicle. The refugees met him with a banner

The graves of the three refugees killed by the Honduran army during the August 1985 attack on Callejón.

Yita, in whose home we stayed for two weeks in August 1989, making tortillas in the vivienda.

demanding an end to the military encirclement and attacks. Turcios responded angrily, trying to run over the banner and refusing to speak with the refugees. They surrounded his car, putting rocks around the tires to prevent him from running over people or leaving. Angered, the Colonel took out his gun and threatened reprisals. The Honduran press, generally hostile to the Salvadoran refugees, claimed that Turcios was attacked by guerrillas in the camp. After the incident, the Honduran foreign minister formally requested that UNHCR move the refugees out of Honduras, and repression in the camp escalated. Threats were made to replace the international agency staff with representatives from CONARE.

Throughout most of 1987, the refugees were forbidden to travel between the subcamps on foot or by vehicle, preventing them from visiting relatives or participating in workshops, committee work, and pastoral activities. No construction materials were allowed into the camp. International workers, with the exception of UNHCR staff and those from MSF (Médecins Sans Frontières, or Doctors Without Borders), were not allowed to stay in the camp overnight, leaving the community more vulnerable to military attacks.

Fredy, in whose home we stayed for two weeks in August 1989, in the entrance to the vivienda.

Providing supplementary food to undernourished children and the elderly in the nutrition center, Quebrachito.

International visitors were prohibited, and a 9:00 P.M. curfew was imposed. The military, both regular territorial troops and U.S.-trained special forces, completely encircled the camp, riding on board every truck that brought supplies into the camp. In that year, there were more than four hundred patrols inside the camp, numerous kidnappings, and three to four hundred incidents of shootings around the camp.

These actions were interpreted by the refugees as calculated to force them to leave the camp, either through "voluntary" repatriation or by relocating to Olanchito. The border area was becoming even more militarized, with new bases under construction and special forces undergoing training there. Hondurans in the area were subject to forced recruitment into the army and were warned not to become involved in pastoral groups, as "this is how things got started in El Salvador."

The repression continued into 1988. On April 23, a sixty-three-year-old refugee working in agriculture at the edge of the camp was fatally shot in

Listening to mass from outside the chapel, Limones.

the back by Honduran soldiers. Stunned by the incident, the refugees rose up in anger and demanded help from UNHCR. "After that," one refugee explained,

> the community got together, and when the Lieutenant came later to acknowledge the death, we weren't afraid, rather we felt strength, and we didn't want him to come in to see the body and we wouldn't let him close to the body. Later a truck full of soldiers came into the camp. But we felt a deep pain, and so the entire community came out into the streets and we had a demonstration, repudiating this assassination. We objected to the soldiers driving through our camp, and the trucks that belonged to the agencies that worked in our community weren't to be used hauling soldiers, and so we made the soldiers get out and walk out of the camp.

The community's strong reaction had an effect: the patrols inside the camp stopped, although soldiers continued to be visible around the perimeter of the camp. Sensing their increased effectiveness in defending themselves through militant action, the refugees launched a hunger strike in June of 1988. This *Ayuno Contra el Hambre y la Represión* (fast against hunger and repression) was targeted at increased cuts in food assistance, persistent shortages in medicine and deteriorating medical treatment, and the continued lack of security and protection. Twenty people participated at first; four days later three hundred had joined in. The *ayuno* ended shortly afterward, when a delegation from UNHCR headquarters in Geneva arrived to discuss improvements in living conditions in the camp and was met by a large, spirited demonstration. These militant expressions had an impact; the community dates their ability to organize free of significant military interference from this point. Inspired by their own success, the refugees later came to see the ayuno as a pivotal event in moving toward self-determination.

However, the violence did not cease entirely. Refugees who were anywhere near the periphery of the camp were likely to be seized by Honduran forces; some were taken when they went to bathe in the quebrada or were gathering fruit or tending crops on the outskirts of the camp. Sometimes these people appeared later, after having been questioned or even tortured; others were never seen again, and their fate was never revealed. About a month before the refugees were to leave for their repatriation to Morazán, two teenage boys disappeared near where gunshots were heard later that night. Their desperate parents were worried that even if the boys were alive, the community would be relocated in their absence. Even in the last days of their status as refugees, the community at Colomoncagua continued to experience hostility and repression.

But the refugees had learned important lessons from these experiences,

Overleaf: Community meetings were an important part of life in the camp. Here people gather for a despedida to send off some visitors.

A community meeting. The sign says, Hands Should Be Washed upon Rising, After Going to the Toilet, and Before Eating.

especially the necessity of militance and solidarity. Their struggles against attacks by the military were successful only when they collectively demanded that no soldiers be permitted to enter the camp: Don't Set Foot in Here! their signs announced, and soldiers who ignored them were mobbed by angry refugees, shouting, "You won't be allowed to kill any more of us!" Sometimes, soldiers who entered were surrounded by women, who addressed them in the familiar *vos* form, as they would speak to their own sons, saying, "You are peasants just like us; we are just like your mothers at home. Why are you doing this to us?" Often, the soldiers, who were in fact peasants like the refugees, would become confused and disturbed. This tactic of personal appeals combined with militant action contributed to the military's decision to withdraw its patrols from within the camp.

Alone, the refugees could not protect their children from kidnappings or their loved ones from harassment or intimidation, but together they could at least restrict the freedom of action of their captors. Their successful six-year campaign to resist forced relocation taught them that they could achieve what they wanted only if they remained steadfast and united.

CHAPTER ▲ THREE

BUILDING THE NEW COMMUNITY

▲▲

> United in pain and anguish and misery, we learned to share the little we had, and to understand what human solidarity means. We left behind a past of misery, oppression, and ignorance; of baseness and evils; and we entered a new stage of living together.

Arriving in Honduras in a matter of days and weeks, hundreds and then thousands of people, mostly complete strangers to one another, found themselves thrust together as refugees, having to share the few resources that were made available to them through the kindness of other strangers. After living their lives dispersed in the countryside—in a little house here or there, at most a cluster of homes making up a *casería* (small village)—the refugees were forced to live cheek to jowl under cramped and confined conditions.

Some refugees become passive in the face of these conditions, totally dependent on the agencies that assist them, or they succumb to the tensions and conflicts that inevitably arise from overcrowding, deprivation, and helplessness. But the refugees at Colomoncagua were able to transcend their situation, drawing from it important lessons about how to live in community.

GOVERNANCE

In those early days, the camp was serviced primarily by Caritas, the international social service arm of the Roman Catholic church. Caritas's philosophy was to promote independence and self-sufficiency as much as possible

Overleaf: A meeting to greet the Salvadoran government delegation visiting Limones in August 1989.

in its work with refugees, unlike some relief agencies, which foster dependency and passivity. The Caritas staff included many social workers, experienced in community organization, who encouraged the refugees to take charge of their own lives as much as possible. Undoubtedly, this had a strong impact on the camp, encouraging a cooperative and democratic spirit.

But that spirit clearly came from the refugees as well. Although most were simple *campesinos*—peasants working the land, living in isolated family units—many had been touched by El Salvador's rich network of popular organizations. Some had been members of Christian base communities, participating in democratic forms of worship and religious community; others had been involved in peasant federations and unions, experiencing firsthand the meaningfulness of collective activity and self-organization. Some had even been activists in revolutionary political groups, bringing to the camp a more sophisticated understanding of organization and leadership. It was not surprising, then, that leaders and organizers emerged readily from the ranks of the refugees, and a vision of a cooperative, egalitarian life-style took root.

Yet, it is important to recognize the extent to which living collectively and managing their own affairs was a remarkable accomplishment for this group of people, some of whom had never before even been to a meeting. A camp document explains: "This has been one of the hardest things for the community to do, to find a mechanism for the coordination of the community. Because we are all peasants, we all lived individually. Everyone looked out for themselves."

A middle-aged man described their transformation from untutored, isolated peasants to citizens of a self-governing community: "When we came here, we were 85 percent illiterate, we had no skills; we knew only how to plant, and not very well at that. Also our cultural level was very low. Now we can say, Who among us would be good at doing this or that? This is the basis of governance." Another refugee added, "In El Salvador, we didn't have any notion of solidarity—everyone prayed to his own saint. But experience taught us differently here."

In the refugees' view, sheer necessity was the main impetus behind the unprecedented level of organization they were to develop in Colomoncagua. The conditions of life in the camp demanded a high degree of cooperation, organization, and leadership. "This is a community that has been considered highly political," explained one leader, "but the issue was really one of efficiency. When you say that the community is political, it sounds like they're responding to larger issues, like support for the FMLN, and not responding to conditions in the community. This community has become conscious of their necessities and that the only way to respond to these necessities is to organize themselves. That's why we're politicized—it's a community conscious of how to resolve its problems."

The preparation of food was the first task to be organized collectively. The refugees had to face the demands of feeding themselves without the individual resources—meager though they had been—that they were used to. As one man put it, "When we came here, we didn't even have utensils to cook with. Caritas donated pots, but they were big ones, so we had to cook collectively. Necessity taught us to do things collectively."

The collective life-style that emerged was both a response to the conditions imposed on the refugees and a deliberate philosophical choice growing out of their experiences as poor people seeking a better life. Imbued with the spiritual values of liberation theology (which we will discuss later), with its emphasis on equality and community, and influenced by those with a more highly developed political consciousness, for whom equality was a political and economic goal, the refugees worked to create a society reflecting their emerging vision of a life radically different from the one they had known in El Salvador.

This meant developing procedures and structures for making decisions, coordinating activities, and allocating resources that were consistent with these values. Through trial and error, through discussion, criticism, and experimentation, the refugees put together an indigenous form of governance that was egalitarian, participatory, and democratic.

The refugees explain this process in one of the documents they wrote:

> When we arrived in Colomoncagua in 1980, one of the new problems we encountered was the need to look for a form of coordination that permitted us to organize the different tasks we faced, such as how to administer the few resources that the humanitarian and solidarity organizations brought us. It was thus that the first form of choosing our representatives was born, in which in open assemblies we chose the first coordinators to direct the work and distribute the food. This was when we were still in the village of Colomoncagua. When we were moved to the camp itself, other necessities and forms of organization presented themselves, which with the passage of time and experience were modified until they reached their present form.

The modification and development of these organizational forms tell us a good deal about how the refugees resolved their problems. As one leader put it, "This community moves forward by experimenting." At first, they established a relatively simple governance structure based on the geographic subdivisions of the refuge into *colonias* (neighborhoods) of about 100 to 125 persons, and subcamps, eventually nine in all, with up to 1,000 people in each. Each colonia and each subcamp elected coordinators and subcoordinators responsible for all aspects of camp life—production, education, sanitation, health, nutrition, construction, and so forth. The subcamp coordinators met as an assembly to represent the needs of the refuge as a whole and to negotiate with UNHCR and other agencies.

The system worked reasonably well for several years, but over time dissatisfactions with inefficiencies and inequities emerged. Since the subcamps were largely autonomous, with control over their own workshops, for example, access to goods and work experiences varied considerably. Bringing together the many coordinators to address refuge-level issues was cumber-

The refugees treated discussions seriously and paid serious attention to each other at meetings.

some, and the leadership was unable to present a united front to UNHCR and other agencies. And because the scope of their responsibilities was so broad, these coordinators did not always have an adequate understanding of all the areas of work or needs. Finally, and perhaps most importantly, participation in decision making was limited, and there were complaints that some coordinators were taking advantage of their considerable personal authority to improve their own positions.

In the spring of 1988, a crisis of sorts was reached. The refugees set in motion a two-month-long process of evaluating the structure and designing a better one. A campaign called Cultural Awakening was launched to

The conjunto plays at civic functions, parties, and religious observances; visitors are welcomed and sent off with community gatherings, which always include music. Felipe (in the hat) lost most of his family in the massacre at Mozote. When he came to the camp, he helped organize the conjunto and teach others to play.

encourage participation in discussions and to mobilize the community to address its problems. Assemblies—Colomoncagua's version of town meetings—were called in colonias, subcamps, and workplaces. Grievances were aired, and suggestions made and discussed. Each coordinator's performance was evaluated by the community, and those found lacking were replaced.

A new, more complex structure—"because our problems are complex"—emerged from this expression of popular will. Refugewide committees were organized around specific areas of need (nutrition, education, construction, and so forth), ensuring more specialized knowledge of each area, greater participation, and better coordination at the level of the refuge as a whole. In a sense, the refugees were learning to think of themselves as a larger unit, an entire population of over eight thousand, moving beyond the more localized, subcamp focus of the previous structure.

As one leader told us, "The internal development of the community was not the only necessary condition for these changes. They also depended on free movement throughout the camp. They were not possible for us when the Honduran military limited travel from one subcamp to another. When they patrolled in the camp, it was impossible to have community meetings." The struggle to defend themselves from military pressures was thus intimately linked to the ongoing political development of the community.

The new organizational structure established an overlapping system of elected and appointed leadership, with a clear division of responsibility and authority. Leaders at the neighborhood level were directly elected; those at the subcamp and refuge level were selected by the lower-level leadership bodies in a pyramidal fashion. All leadership was collective rather than individual, and areas of responsibility were divided among different committees with clear authority and considerable autonomy, so that no one group—or individual—ran the whole camp.

A member of a high-level committee explained the checks and balances of this system of governance:

> If you are a leader, it's pretty hard to come out good every time. But doing it our way, we have the advantage of being able to resolve problems of the community more easily. And in this way the community really benefits from all that it produces. One group isn't going to get more and another group less. . . . If someone tries to take advantage, there is someone else there to say that isn't right. And so the representatives see that they should do things in the right way. Also, the representatives suffer the same problems as everyone else, and so they feel and know that the needs are the needs of all, not just a few. So decisions are made to favor all of the people. The community sees it that way too; everyone is in need. And so they have confidence in their representatives to do things properly.

The formal governance structure that finally evolved in Colomoncagua was as follows (see organizational chart in appendix A): Each colonia held an assembly to elect people to be responsible for different areas of service and administration. This group made up the Comité de Colonia, the neighborhood-level leadership body. Colonia leaders from the entire subcamp got together by work area and elected one person from each area to make up the subcamp leadership body, the Comité Comunal.

The leadership structure for the refuge as a whole, the Comité Comunal del Refugio, was composed of one representative from each of the nine subcamp Comités Comunales. This group then named refugewide committees to be responsible for different work areas: education, production and distribution, health, food, and so forth. These work committees meeting as a group constituted the body with the highest authority in the camp, the Asamblea de Comités. Since this very large group could not easily meet very often, a Comisión Coordinadora was formed to handle day-to-day decisions, made up of one representative from each work committee and one representative for all the subcamp Comités Comunales.

The Asamblea de Comités also selected members of a special body, the Comité de Relaciones, whose important job was to deal with external organizations, such as UNHCR, relief organizations, governments, visitors, and the like. One member of this committee was also appointed to the Comisión Coordinadora.

Terms of office for all these positions were two years, although people might serve for more than one term if they functioned well and could be (and were) recalled if there was dissatisfaction.

A unique feature of the new governance structure was what the refugees called "sectors." The subcamps were divided into demographic groups—women, men, youth, children, and war-disabled—which met regularly to discuss issues of concern to the community as a whole or of specific concern to that sector. (Sometimes the pastoral groups were also described as sectors, although these were actually independent of the governance apparatus.)

Through these multiple structures, every person in the camp, every man, woman, and child, belonged to several different constituencies—the colonia, the subcamp, the workplace, the sector—and in this way had many opportunities to participate in the community's deliberations. The links between the individual and the community were strengthened through these multiple and overlapping layers of interaction and involvement.

As might be expected from this complex and tightly knit organization, meetings took place all the time—in colonias and subcamps, in workshops and other work sites, among the sectoral and pastoral groups, in work committees, and among all levels of leadership. These frequent meetings increased involvement at the same time that they fostered cohesiveness and unity. People at the grass roots had many opportunities to influence the leadership, and vice versa.

Decision making in the camp was generally an open and fluid process, involving considerable discussion by people at all levels. An example of this openness was seen when the refugees were planning the move from Colomoncagua to Meanguera. A construction task force was developed to organize the building of the dwellings in the new settlement. The decision about what these houses would look like involved numerous discussions within the entire community, with much give-and-take by many parties, grass roots and leadership alike. Meetings of those responsible for planning the move were open, and members of the construction task force would drop in and offer their suggestions. To encourage broad input and participation a model home was built in one of the subcamps.

One afternoon, a group of women and children gathered to talk with some members of the construction crew.

"Do you like where we put the window?"

"The window is ok, but there is a more serious problem. You didn't put in a back door. We need a back door."

Meetings were frequently called to listen to readings of news reports monitored from various radio stations. Later, the meetings were replaced by afternoon readings over a public-address system in each subcamp.

In case of attack by the Salvadoran military, there would be no escape route. The construction group agreed with the criticism, and a back door was added. A similar change, intended to save materials and time, was made in the design of the roof.

The balance achieved by this unique organizational structure between effectiveness and efficiency on the one hand, and democracy and participation on the other, was impressive. While the process of electing higher-level bodies was somewhat indirect, leadership was varied, visible, and accountable, with little separation between leaders and the grass roots. Those in leadership positions worked hard and received few tangible privileges; they were just as poor as everyone else, living in the same circumstances and equally vulnerable to the decisions they made for the community as a whole.

Furthermore, there was considerable opportunity for participation and

Distributing cooking oil to the families in Callejón.

input by the community at large. This entailed considerable effort and learning because the refugees had little experience managing their own affairs or
expressing their own views before coming to the camp. Their inexperience,
passivity, and well-founded caution, shaped by generations of poverty and
repression, were not easily overcome. One man described the change in this
way: "Before, very few would speak. The rest would sit at meetings like
iguanas, nodding our heads and agreeing. Now people have learned to pro-
pose things, present their ideas. Now there is a lot more discussion." He
went on to explain that back in El Salvador disputes would often be settled
with violence (typically the result of drinking) or through intervention by

external authorities, such as a local mayor, who would impose a fine or some other punishment. "Here, we've come to see discussion as a way of resolving problems."

▲　　　　▲　　　　▲

We are meeting with the Nutrition Committee, which is responsible for ensuring an adequate and fair distribution of food for the refuge as a whole. The seven people, three men and four women, sit around a small table. Two of the women have young children with them; one, an infant, nurses from time to time during the discussion. We ask them to explain how the decision was reached to kill some of the hens when UNHCR cut back feed. Our purpose is to get a clear sense of who has the authority to make important decisions in the community, the work committees or the broader leadership bodies.

"We look at the problem, discuss it among ourselves, in community. Then we take proposals to the Comisión Coordinadora, which is a bigger body, and every committee has a member on it, including us. The comisión approves the proposal." The woman who is speaking clarifies what she has just said: "Every committee has autonomy; they make the decision. The decision with the hens went like this. The agency worker suggested that we kill two-thirds of the hens. We discussed this and decided it was a good idea. Then we made a report to the comisión—not to be told what to do, but for consultation. The decision was made by the committee."

The woman with the infant holds him up so that he can pee on the dirt floor. We press the issue further: "Suppose there were a conflict; let's say the comisión wanted to kill only half of the hens. What would happen then?"

"So far that situation hasn't happened. If it did, we'd listen to them and look for another way to do it. But it's really our decision."

▲　　　　▲　　　　▲

The activities of the colonia coordinator illustrate the unique social roles that were developed in Colomoncagua to foster the communitarian life-style of the camp. Luisa is a young mother of three who served for four years as a colonia coordinator in one of Colomoncagua's nine subcamps. She was responsible for a neighborhood of about a dozen households. Working as part of a team with the other colonia coordinators in the subcamp, Luisa functioned essentially as a social worker/community organizer, ensuring that responsibilities were carried out satisfactorily, that residents' needs were met, and that discussion was facilitated. If people were not doing their work adequately, she would talk with them and see what the problem was. Often the solution was simply to persuade them how important it was that the work get done; other times, it may have been possible to find a new, more satisfactory job assignment.

Learning to make jewelry out of various kinds of native seeds in a crafts training workshop.

"Let's say I notice someone who doesn't want to work," she explained, "someone who seems discouraged and stays apart from people. So I talk to them, try to find out what the problem is. I explain that if they don't express what the problem is, they'll just keep feeling it. I try to encourage them to work." And what if the individual feels unfairly treated? "Maybe the problem is that they saw things distributed and they felt they didn't get their share. They could be feeling resentful. If I find out about it I can talk to them, explain what the reasons are. Also, I point out that if they're angry and don't go to work and others do the same, we'll have fewer people working and even less to distribute."

▲   ▲   ▲

The success of this tightly knit model of social organization was due in large measure to the special circumstances of the refugees' experience of exile. First of all, the group was extremely homogeneous: all from the same general area in rural El Salvador; virtually all Catholic; all poor and under-educated, arriving at the camp with minimal personal possessions, no special privileges to preserve or extend, and shared experiences of terror and victimization.

Second, the refugees were united by a common enemy, the Honduran military, which treated them as dangerous subversives, holding them in captivity and intruding aggressively on numerous occasions. The years-long threat of forced relocation by the Honduran government drew the refugees into a defensive posture, forcing them to struggle for their own survival.

Third, the success the refugees had in defending themselves and securing improvement in their living condition through collective action was in itself an important factor in propelling them further. Campesinos often have a fatalistic view of life, an acceptance of whatever terrible things come their way—which can make them resilient in the face of hardship, but can also lead them to be passive. In Colomoncagua that passivity was stripped away, and a more assertive consciousness took its place. Each threat that was

Refugee Poster: To Defend Our Rights, We Organized

challenged, each advance that was made, represented a further step in the growing confidence that the refugees could determine their own fate—but only if they were united and organized.

Of course, there were some in the community who were uncomfortable with the constant calls for unity and participation, who rejected the collective path that was so strongly urged by community leaders. About fifty families and perhaps a few dozen individuals left the camp, some to repatriate individually, others to seek refuge in other countries such as Canada, and still others to form a separate refugee community—this one not restricted by the Honduran military—in the town of Colomoncagua. The refugees complained that UNHCR continually tried to encourage people to leave the camp individually, offering them money to repatriate; UNHCR alleged that people came to them at night, saying that they wanted to leave but were afraid of retribution by camp leaders.

The circumstances of exile, especially the military encirclement but also the background of violence and fear imposed by civil war and repression, meant that the community in Colomoncagua was forged in an artificial and distorted climate. That democracy and decency were able to flourish at all in the midst of these conditions is testimony to the unique spirit of the people in the camp. What they were able to accomplish under these trying conditions was genuinely impressive.

EDUCATION

> "Education had a lot to do with the communitarian way of thinking. . . . The fact of being educated develops the person and makes them think in a new way. To be in complete ignorance, not to know even how to read or write your own name, not to be able to pick up a book. . . ."

Perhaps the refugees' proudest accomplishment is in the area of education. Arriving at the camp about 85 percent illiterate, the refugees turned that figure around during their stay in Colomoncagua. Lacking trained teachers at first, the few who were able to read and write began to teach the many who could not. "There was no agency that helped us but that wasn't an obstacle," the refugees have written, "because with high morale and with the little that we knew, we shared all with the whole community. Under the trees, we wrote with coal on pieces of cardboard, the *compañeros* who knew how to write a few sentences teaching the others how to do it."

Later, Caritas responded to their requests for assistance and sent volunteers to train teachers and set up literacy classes for adults and primary schools for children. Throughout their stay in the camp, the refugees took steps to ensure that they, and not outsiders, were the teachers for their own community. Thus, the foreigners (mostly Caritas volunteers from Europe but some Hondurans as well) ran the teacher training programs, while the refugees ran the schools. This became an area of struggle in 1987, when the

Reading a newspaper brought by a visitor. Any reading material brought into the camp was eagerly read by the newly literate refugees.

Honduran government complained that there were no formally trained or certified teachers in the camp, and announced that one hundred Hondurans would be sent to teach primary school there. The refugees effectively resisted this plan, arguing that they had succeeded very well in educating themselves and suggesting that the money would be better spent by sending those teachers into the countryside of Honduras, where they were sorely needed.

Over and over, when asked where they learned to read and write, the refugees responded with pride, "Here, in the camp." "When I came here, I knew only one letter, the letter *c*," admitted a leader of the Congregation of Christian Men for Peace, who had just given a graceful reading of passages from the Bible to his group. "We didn't go to school much in El Salvador because we had to work, or because we were too poor and couldn't pay for books. Or the school was too far away," an older man explained. An elderly couple who had both learned to read in the camp and now liked to read for pleasure lamented that there just weren't enough books available: "Now we have a need for books because we can read."

The accomplishments in literacy were tangible: people throughout the camp could be seen using their new skills daily—writing things down in little notebooks at meetings, reading newspapers and leaflets (sometimes mouthing the words aloud, as new readers often do), taking notes or reading manuals at their workplaces. There were signs posted throughout the camp: political slogans on banners and posters; notices of all kinds tacked on the walls, indoors and outside. Workshops had handmade signs listing the rules about safety and cleanliness, about being responsible and working collectively. Reading and writing were clearly functional skills that were used in the camp, so that what was learned in the classroom could be put into practice and reinforced in daily life.

Just about everybody in Colomoncagua was a student of some kind, and education involved more than just literacy training. Schools were set up for children through sixth grade and for adults through fifth grade. The curriculum was a full one: social studies, natural science, mathematics, and Spanish language. Classes for children took place a half-day every weekday, and for adults weekday evenings, or during the afternoon for those whose eyesight required better light. (Most evening classes relied on smoky kerosene lamps, and even classrooms that had electricity were lighted by one bare bulb in the center of the room.) Teachers, many of them just barely teenagers, would attend teacher-training classes before or after school, learning the material just a step ahead of their pupils. It was not uncommon to see adults and children alike doing their homework at their little tables in their homes at night by the light of a kerosene lamp, or sitting on their doorstep during the day, with a notebook and pencil, doing sums or writing out their lessons.

Like most effective literacy campaigns in so-called Third World countries, the refugees in Colomoncagua used techniques drawn from the famed Brazilian educator Paolo Freire. Simply put, his approach uses key words that come from the experience of the learner and provide a basis for a dialogue between learner and teacher. This process entails a change in consciousness, not just the acquisition of skills, which Freire saw as necessary for overcoming the barriers to adult literacy. This approach is markedly different from ones which use words chosen primarily for their phonetic characteristics and which rely on a more traditional relationship between teacher and learner.

In the camp, the word *refugiado* (refugee) was a useful one for teaching people to read because of its obvious resonance of meaning and the additional advantage that it contained all the vowels. However, its length made it difficult for beginners. For this reason, a modified Freirian technique was developed, and simpler words were chosen that were not so ideal semantically, but were useful for grasping the basics of phonetics.

While adult education was heavily influenced by Freire, schooling for children in the camp was more traditional. To a large extent this reflected the refugees' tendency to recreate whatever educational experiences they had had in the country schools of El Salvador, where children sit passively on benches and teachers point at syllables and words written on the blackboard, leading them in shouting, repetitive drills. The international volunteers from Caritas tried to encourage the refugees to develop more flexible and modern classroom techniques—discussions and games, individualized lessons, emphasis on conceptualization rather than memorization, and so forth—but the more familiar approach seemed to win out.

A typical elementary school class.

Interestingly, adults in Colomoncagua had an easier time learning to read and write than children did, quite the reverse of experiences with adult literacy programs in the United States. In the camp, adults were highly motivated: the refugees saw literacy as a right that they had to fight for, and understood its significance for their individual and collective development. And their learning was reinforced by the many opportunities to use their new skills: they could read the many publications that were produced in the camp, they could participate more effectively at meetings, and they could learn other skills that were dependent on basic literacy. Finally, the whole community was learning together, with the day's activities organized so as to give time for schooling.

For the children, on the other hand, motivation was more uneven. The classrooms were noisy and uncomfortable, with hard benches and dirt floors, and the kids were distracted by competing activities, including, of course, play. The old-fashioned teaching style, with its emphasis on shouted recitation, failed to maintain the interest of all the pupils or to detect children who were having difficulties. As a result, a large number—more than half in some years—had to repeat first grade and were delayed in picking up the rudiments of reading.

Other factors contributed to this problem. Although most children spent two years in *kinder* (preschool) before entering first grade, they didn't receive any real preparation for schooling there, largely because the women who staffed the program were not trained as educators. And even though most of the children's parents were now literate, they were unable to transfer their skills effectively to their children because of the lack of children's books to read with them. The impoverished conditions in the camp—lack of suitable and attractive reading material for children, inadequate lighting, cramped living areas—were a significant barrier for children learning to read. Also, kids spent most of their time, when they weren't in school or in the workshops, playing with each other in the "streets," and this distracted them from their lessons.

Yet the advances the refugees made in education for children and adults alike are indeed impressive. Coming from a country in which schooling was a luxury for most people in the countryside, the refugees at Colomoncagua firmly established the right of all people, young and old, to learn, and made education a central part of their lives. The community also effectively bridged the generation gap between teachers and learners. It was not unusual to see a youth of fifteen instructing a group ranging in age from twenty to sixty. And they developed a cadre of trained teachers—nearly four hundred of them—who will play an invaluable role in a region that had fewer than two dozen teachers before the refugees relocated there.

Education in Colomoncagua went beyond literacy programs, preschools and primary schools, and teacher-training programs. The refugees ran their own technical school to provide more advanced instruction in specialized areas. Here women and men studied mechanical drawing, typing, art, busi-

Children in a guardería.

ness administration, geometry, and basic principles of mechanics, electricity, and chemical science. Education also encompassed a lively and well-organized program of sports in the camp, with leagues of men's and women's teams (soccer for men, European handball for women), complete with uniforms (donated by international agencies), referees, and championship matches. (A few of the men could be seen playing soccer with an arm missing, a reminder of the war that always lurked in the background.) The educational program also provided instruction and performance in music and theater, and workshops for children and adults in handicrafts and toymaking.

▲   ▲   ▲

In the technical training school, the middle-aged man in charge proudly shows us the library. There are about fifty books and pamphlets on the shelf, not a very generous collection but far beyond what most of these people had ever encountered. Most were donated by agency staff; some were produced and duplicated in the camp. The *responsable* (person in charge) takes one such document off the shelf, a mimeographed manual for the intermediate mechanical drawing course. He shows it to us with a mixture of shyness and pride. At the bottom of the title page are the words, "Hecho Por Daniel" (made by Daniel).

"But you are Daniel, aren't you?"

"Yes, I wrote the text."

"Where did you learn to do that?"

"An international volunteer came here and taught elementary mechanical drawing. I took that course. The international left us some more advanced books, so I read them, so I could teach others. And I wrote our texts."

"Did you do this kind of work before, in El Salvador?"

"No, I learned it all here."

In the next room a small group (four men and two women) is learning about ferric metals. On the walls are colorful charts explaining the structure of automobile engines and radiators, and a handmade chart identifying different types of tools. In another room a young woman writes on the blackboard, while her students, three women and a man, copy in their notebooks what she has written. This is a class in business administration, and the sentences on the board are about maintaining and controlling inventories: "Make sure materials are well protected from the climate." "Study the

A class in the technical school.

The auto mechanics class in the technical school.

guides for taking care of each material.'' Down the hall two men are working quietly together at problems in long division.

One of the very special achievements of the refugees while they were in
Colomoncagua was to set up a rudimentary library. An international volunteer from Germany contributed his little house and books when he left the
camp, and the community slowly accumulated more. The library was a
place where people could come to read or to take a book out on loan, for one
week. The project was just under way when the refugees made their decision
to return to El Salvador, so they knew that it wouldn't really get off the
ground until they moved. "This might not be a big thing in the history of the

camp," admitted the elderly man in charge of the project. "Maybe it'll be here just a few months. But we'll establish the *idea* of a library, which people will want when they go back," he added proudly. "When we go there [to El Salvador] and set up this library, it's going to be admired by the people there, a sign of what we've learned."

HEALTH

> "For the first time, we came to understand the main factors that cause malnourishment among poor people, and the way to combat this infirmity."

In rural El Salvador, health care is truly a privilege, not a right. As in most Third World countries, few doctors live or work in the countryside, and there is no adequate formal system of public health care. People get sick and die of diseases that are easily preventable or curable, and poverty contributes to a generally low level of physical and mental well-being.

In Colomoncagua, despite limited health care personnel and supplies, the refugees probably had greater attention paid to their health than ever before. Moreover, while in the camp they learned how to take care of themselves in order to prevent disease, and a cadre of health paraprofessionals was trained to maintain the health of the community and even to treat illness.

Starting in 1984, health care in Colomoncagua was provided by the French humanitarian organization, Médecins Sans Frontières (Doctors Without Borders). MSF provided a rotating staff of a doctor, a midwife, and two nurses. They set up two clinics in the camp, one for each zone, with a small laboratory in each clinic. The medical staff lived in the town of Colomoncagua, not in the camp itself, and was also responsible for the twelve hundred refugees at San Antonio, roughly an hour and a half away during the dry season and a longer ride in the rainy season. The one doctor, therefore, was responsible for approximately ten thousand persons in two locations. While praising MSF for its dedication, the refugees complained that often sick people went unattended because staffing was inadequate. Moreover, if patients needed hospitalization, they had to be taken by road and small plane to Tegucigalpa, a half-day's trip that required crossing several military checkpoints. Often the military would interrogate the patients, accusing them of being guerrillas and interfering with their care.

To provide a more permanent system for responding to their health needs, the refugees set up a parallel structure consisting of a refugee-run health care center in each subcamp, staffed by four persons plus another assigned as a kind of health outreach worker for each colonia. These paramedical health outposts took care of routine health matters, bringing patients to the doctor's attention when necessary. They dispensed medicines such as aspirin, antacids, antidiarrhea and antiparasite compounds, and even antibiotics; at-

In addition to the work crews who cleaned out the latrines daily, there were frequent mobilizations to sweep and clean areas of the camp.

tended to minor injuries and ailments; assisted in childbirths; weighed and measured infants; and kept statistics and records. Responding broadly to community needs, these health care workers would make home visits, provide follow-up care for recuperating patients, and offer patient education—explaining, for example, the results of lab tests and giving nutritional advice to pregnant and nursing women. The outreach workers would begin each day by going from house to house to see if anyone needed medical attention, so that illnesses were detected before they become serious.

Originally, MSF cooperated in this parallel structure, helping to establish it and providing training and assistance, including supplies of medicines and other resources. But the doctors were always somewhat reluctant to train refugees as health care providers or have them attend consultations. Finally, by 1988, the organization withdrew its support from the outreach program altogether. This withdrawal of support seems to have been a reflection of a conservative philosophical and political shift that occurred in top-level MSF leadership in France at that time and the traditional assumption that the doctor's purpose was to treat the patient, not teach the community. Some individual doctors in the camp continued to give assistance, but there was no longer a regular program of training for indigenous health care personnel in the camp. The refugees were forced to rely on written materials, particularly the book *Donde No Hay Doctor* (Where there is no doctor), a text written by a North American, David Werner, for "barefoot doctors" and used widely throughout the Third World.

The strain between the refugees and MSF grew into a significant political conflict, a product of the community's growing capability and self-confidence. The refugee health workers complained that the doctors distrusted them, giving them few responsibilities, denying medicine and equipment for their centers, and doubting information they provided about the patients. Tension mounted; MSF accused the refugees of diverting medicine to the guerrillas, promoting a climate of control and hostility, and deliberately preventing refugees from seeking care from the professional staff, in order later to be able to claim mistreatment. The refugees, for their part, complained that

In digging a new latrine, as in most areas of life, children and adults worked together.

MSF had taken on a negative and insensitive attitude toward them, and blamed inadequate treatment by MSF doctors for the deaths of many refugees. They documented their claims with clinical records and testimony from numerous patients.

"Since 1987, I've been seeing the doctors," reads the testimony of a 101-year-old woman, "and finally the doctor told me, 'I'm not going to give you medicine, because you've already lived a long time, and are very old. Old people like you don't need medical attention.'" A 20-year-old woman being treated for a long-standing heart condition states: "The doctors told me that I was a guerrilla, and I should give the names of my family members. They really terrified me." Two other young women recounted that "the MSF doctors told us that there was nothing wrong with us, that all we needed was to get a husband."

By August of 1988, the refugees were calling for UNHCR to cease its contractual arrangement with MSF and expel the organization from the camp. Intense negotiations between the refugee leadership and UNHCR went on for several months, with UNHCR largely defending MSF's performance in the camp and the refugees insisting that a more suitable agency be found to administer to their health needs. When MSF's contract expired in December of that year, the organization officially withdrew from the camp, although it had effectively cut its ties earlier. After that time, health care was taken over by the Honduran Ministry of Public Health.

The refugees were pleased with the care provided by the Honduran medical professionals, and found their attitude more sympathetic. However, the basic problems of health in the camp were not resolved. Inadequate diet, poor living conditions, the stress of confinement, and shortages in basic medicines continued to take their toll in unnecessary human suffering. An infant crying inconsolably because there was no aspirin in the camp to relieve the pain of an ear infection, a young woman limited in her activities because of chronic, and treatable, anemia, an elderly man unable to read because eyeglasses were not available, almost all adults with teeth missing because of the lack of dental care and a diet that was too soft—the list of avoidable miseries is endless.

Health care is not just a matter of curing disease; prevention is undoubtedly equally important. While in the camp, the refugees learned a great deal about keeping themselves healthy through proper sanitation and hygiene. The overcrowded conditions in Colomoncagua demanded exacting attention to these matters. On first glance, the residences resembled the urban slums so common throughout Latin America: jumbled shacks with corrugated tin roofs; no sewers, running water, or electricity; a hot climate that turned the ground into dust for half the year and mud the other half; mobs of children running about, many of them barefoot; chickens roaming freely and an occasional cow or two wandering among the dwellings, especially at night, leaving behind piles of excrement. But unlike other poor, densely populated towns and cities of Latin America, Colomoncagua was very clean.

Sanitation was an important area of work in the camp, and committees on the colonia and subcamp level took responsibility to ensure that the streets and alleys were swept free of trash and animal droppings, latrines were cleaned thoroughly each day, and garbage was collected and properly burned.

▲   ▲   ▲

Don Andrés is a man in his mid-sixties, a *sobador* (folk masseur). After a number of years in the workshops of the camp, he switched to sanitation—cleaning and washing latrines.
"How do you find the work?"
"Oh, I like it."
"But how can you *like* cleaning the latrines?"
"Because I know that it's something for the good of the community."

▲   ▲   ▲

The community learned about sterilizing drinking water and washing hands as means of preventing illness. Every household had its own jug of boiled water, carefully covered by a cloth to keep out flies. People usually washed before eating, scooping up a bit of water from a large barrel kept outside the home to rinse off the crude soap. Most of them had never known the luxury of indoor plumbing, and keeping themselves clean was not a serious problem except in the dry season when water was scarce. Women would often bathe at the same time they washed clothes, in the little streams and pools that would fill up during the rainy season (and never quite run out in the dry season) in the quebrada that ran through the center of the camp, or at one of the pilas supplied by the UN-sponsored water system. They were not shy about baring their breasts there (after all, they nursed their babies quite openly), but they kept their slips on so they could wash without revealing too much of their bodies. Men preferred to bathe in greater privacy in a more remote part of the quebrada.

The only serious unaddressed hygiene problem in the camp was the ubiquitous habit of spitting, a practice common to rural Salvadorans. Even young children, girls as well as boys, learn to spit forcefully and loudly. Spitting took place indoors or out, at meetings and social events, apparently becoming more intense when people were nervous or agitated. It seemed as common and natural for them as yawning or clearing our throats is for us. Yet it is a health hazard, since saliva is a source of spreading infection, but in Colomoncagua there were no posters informing people of the problem in the same way that handwashing or latrine use was promoted.

Another area of preventive health that the refugees successfully addressed was nutrition. Staff from Caritas and UNHCR took responsibility for ensuring that their diet was adequate, and taught about nutritional requirements

Young girls in a workshop in Colomoncagua.

Young boys in a workshop in Colomoncagua.

for preventing disease and improving health. Refugee-run committees at the subcamp and refuge level were selected to plan and administer for dietary needs, and nutrition became an important work area.

In May of 1981, under the direction of two North American women, both trained nutritionists, the community established two nutrition centers, one in each zone of the camp, staffed by a team of twelve men and women. To do this, they had to overcome some skepticism by the camp coordinators, who knew little about the significance of nutrition and the extent of nutritional disorders in the camp. The initial focus of the program was on children. A census of all children up to age six was taken, and three levels of malnutrition were identified; the first two required supplementing the normal diet, and the third was serious enough to require a special diet altogether.

The staff in the nutrition centers took responsibility for developing supplemental diets for all the refugees in their care, children and adults alike, identifying a suitable ration of fruits, vegetables, meat, eggs, and dairy products to improve their health. After some prodding, UNHCR provided assistance for these efforts and helped to establish nutrition centers in six subcamps. A French nutritionist was provided by Caritas.

The gardens planted in terraces along the rocky hillside of the camp and the hens and rabbits kept in the community *granjas* (barns) provided small quantities of supplemental vegetables and meat and considerable numbers of eggs for the community. (Many families had a few chickens that roosted in their kitchens or in small coops outside their homes and ran about freely among the dwellings, providing individual households with additional eggs.) A portion of the collectively produced food was diverted to the nutrition centers before the rest was divided among the population. However, the poor quality of the soil and the lack of water during the dry season (half the year) made this a very limited source.

A view of some of the terraced hortalizas, which provided work as well as variety in the refugees' diet.

The nutrition centers kept track of how much food was made available to the population in the camp as a whole, noting inadequacies, responding to cutbacks, and generally pressuring UNHCR for a more adequate diet. They also provided nutritional education for the refugees, giving *charlas* (talks) on diet and health.

During the first year or so of their operation, the nutrition centers were well stocked, allowing the staff to cure seventy-six people with tuberculosis and ensure that pregnant women and nursing mothers received sufficient supplementary food. The refugees had learned a great deal about how to address their own nutritional problems and those of poor people in general. But in 1983, UNHCR, claiming that malnourishment had ended, cut back support for the nutrition centers, and the nutritionists from abroad left the camp. The refugees pressed to keep the centers open, and after six months of stalemate, UNHCR proposed that supplemental food be bought by the medical team in the camp. Between 1984 and 1987, the centers stayed open, but had much fewer resources; it was not until 1987 that supplementary rations for pregnant women could again be provided. But these were cut again in 1988.

In that year, supplies for the nutrition centers were cut back again, so that only those who were assigned there by the doctors could be provided with extra food. For others, a supplemental diet was available only by taking away a portion of the rations of the whole community. By the time the refugees were about to leave, at the end of 1989, only malnourished children and the elderly were receiving additional food.

The general amount and variety of food supplied to the camp by UNHCR was always a concern of the refugees. Sometimes the problem was that the people were not accustomed to certain foods (such as milk or canned sardines, for example), or that they were given a kind of bean (a staple for them) that they didn't like. More typically, especially in the later years of their stay in Colomoncagua (and apparently escalating dramatically once the refugees had announced their intention to repatriate), the problem was that the diet provided for them was terribly limited in both quantity and variety. The refugees complained bitterly that in El Salvador, as poor as they had

The pig granja, where pigs were raised for meat.

been, they were able to take advantage of the wide variety of fruits and vegetables available in the countryside. In the camp, however, their diet was limited to corn (for tortillas), beans, and rice, with very little meat, eggs, cheese, condiments, or fruits and vegetables. Their ration of meat, for example, was four ounces per month—just enough, they said, to remind the children what it tasted like. This restricted diet not only led to malnourishment, it also took away their appetite and depressed them considerably.

"In El Salvador, we had beef three times a week," a refugee who worked in the barnyards complained. "Here, we haven't had any beef in years. [There] we could get lots of fruits and vegetables—mangoes, watermelons, cantaloupes, pineapple. Here, no. The kids grow up without ever having tasted them."

WORKSHOPS

> "The idea is when we arrive in our country, to take advantage of everything we've been able to learn here. Because this has been a school for us; it's been a development for all of us."

Capacitación (training or developing skills) is a key word for the community, since it signifies the extent to which the refugees became capable and confident during their stay in Colomoncagua. Most of them arrived knowing little beyond rudimentary agricultural practices (for men) and the preparation of tortillas and other foods (for women). During their period of exile they learned a wide range of skills, taught to them initially by those refugees with some specialized knowledge or by personnel from the international agencies; these skills were then passed on within the camp from one refugee to another. In this way the refugees became capable of taking care of their needs and developing their potential as individuals and as a community. "Here we like to share," explained the responsable of the shoemaking workshop. "Everyone who learns something likes to share it with someone else."

The refugees were frank in describing how underdeveloped they had been before coming to Colomoncagua. "Before, we didn't know anything, even how to plant vegetables. Here, every kid knows what fertilizer to use for each plant. We didn't know how to administer. How many of us knew how to make things? It used to be, we'd go to the big towns and see things that were manufactured—we didn't know anything about how they were made, not even knitting." "Back in El Salvador, we might see socks for sale at the market. We didn't even know where they came from, much less how they were made. And now we make them," one refugee added with evident pride. The backwardness of women was even more dramatic. As one woman, a member of a high-level leadership body, put it: "Campesino women never saw money—they wouldn't even recognize a peso. They were illiterate and ignorant."

During their stay in Colomoncagua, the refugees established a broad set of workshops, which functioned both as training and production sites. The

Weaving braids of palm leaves, which will later be sewn into hats, in the hatmaking workshop.

agency providing most of the assistance in this area was Catholic Relief Services. Its staff trained the refugees, secured the equipment and materials (e.g., sewing machines, cloth, lathes, tools, sheet metal), and gave technical assistance. The work was organized, supervised, and carried out by the refugees themselves. The workshops were coordinated by the refuge-level committee in charge of distribution and production, with a responsable selected for each workshop by the leadership on the basis of their skills, work, and dedication. A large number of the responsables were women.

By the time they were ready to return to El Salvador, the refugees were

In a costura workshop.

Learning manualidad—embroidery, in this case—in a crafts training workshop.

producing almost all the goods used in the camp: shoes, pottery, hammocks, musical instruments, furniture, soccer balls, tools such as machetes and knives, tin buckets, woven bags, clothing (including knitted sweaters, caps, and socks), straw hats, and a variety of handicrafts, such as carved wooden animals, toy trucks and cars, embroidered napkins and cloths, and traditional jewelry made of seeds and other materials. Some of these items, especially the handicrafts and hammocks, were available for purchase by visitors, with the proceeds going to the community.

The workshops were real workplaces, opening at 8:00 A.M. and closing at 4:00 P.M., with an hour's break for lunch, operating six days a week. The work was taken seriously because people knew that they would be using the products and because they derived pleasure from learning the skills. The workshops received requests for goods from the *almacén,* the central warehouse where the products were stored and then distributed to the subcamps, although there were no individual production quotas set. Children worked in most of the workshops, and some were especially staffed by youngsters: handicrafts, embroidery (mostly by girls), and hatmaking (by boys). Everybody in the camp who was able was expected to perform work of some sort and was encouraged to choose the kind of job they wanted to do. The community had to ensure that all the necessary tasks got done, so if a particular

In the fábrica de zapatos in Quebracho.

workplace needed more volunteers, people were recruited to do the job. They might stay with one kind of work for a long time, or try something new when they wished, depending on whether space was available.

In the camp, work was unpaid, and no record was kept of how much time each person put in. People did not work for wages to support themselves or to win advantages for their families; they worked for the good of the community, so that everyone's needs would be met. Goods were distributed entirely on a per capita or per household basis, not according to how much work the individual had done. However, if someone was not doing their fair share, the appropriate responsable would talk to them about the problem.

The workshop that crafted musical instruments, supplying violins, guitars, and string basses for the camp's band, had been started by an older refugee who had brought his violin with him to the camp, and taught others how to build them. He had been assisted by a refugee from San Antonio, who was allowed by the Honduran authorities to visit Colomoncagua for a few days and give instruction there. The pottery workshop, too, used the skills that refugees brought with them to the camp. In this case, it was an older woman who knew traditional handbuilding techniques and shapes for clay vessels and pots, useful for cooking and as water containers. Her own skills were enhanced by an instructor from Honduras who taught her and others how to throw pots on a foot-operated potter's wheel.

Generally the pace of work was relatively relaxed and informal, so much so that CRS staff were concerned that when the refugees returned to El Salvador, they would have to press themselves harder and set more stringent

In the fábrica de zapatos in Quebracho.

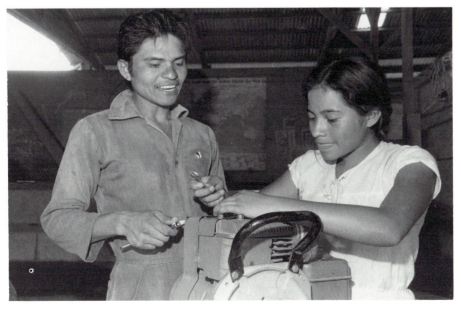

Repairing a small gasoline motor in the mechanical workshop.

Water vessels and other utensils were made on kick wheels in the ceramics workshop.

production goals in order to be economically self-sufficient. The leadership was aware of the problem. Discussions were held in workshops to prepare for what things would be like when they returned.

▲   ▲   ▲

At a tailoring workshop, the workers—mostly women but also a few young men—sat quietly, their machines still, as the responsable told them: "We have to think about how we'll be working there [in Meanguera]. Maybe we'll work from seven to twelve, and then break for lunch. We'll need eight hours of work, a full work day; people can't just come when they want." She paused and suggested, "Maybe someone else has ideas to share." No one spoke, so she continued. "The first thing we'll have to do there is build houses. Maybe it'll be six months before we can start working in the

Opposite: In the camp, many of the instruments, including violins and basses, were made in the workshops.

workshops. We won't have training there so we have to take advantage of the time we have here now." She paused, and again encouraged others to speak, in the way most leaders in the camp tended to do: "This is my idea, but you should say what you think."

A young man taking a break from his work in the mechanics shop was asked if life was difficult in the camp for young people. "No, not really," he replied. "We have lots of work to do here. The only thing that's boring is that we don't have any place to go." His eyes gazed at the distant hills in his homeland, not far away but unreachable. "It gets boring to pass through the same places every day and never to be able to leave the camp."

WOMEN

"It's good now that the women as well as the men are constructing.
We all work in one project, everyone working equally."

A middle-aged woman from Washington, D.C., returning from a religious delegation to Colomoncagua in December 1989, commented enthusiastically, "I've never seen so many empowered women in all my life!" Even to North American eyes, the women in Colomoncagua had gone a long way toward emancipating themselves from traditional gender restrictions, and by Central American standards their gains were quite remarkable.

Women outnumbered men by almost two to one in the camp, and most households were female-headed, not surprising facts in a population ravaged by poverty and war. One might assume that it was the absence of men that gave women room to play a fuller role in the life of the community, but this would be too simple an explanation. Instead, a fortuitous combination of social upheaval, revolutionary idealism, and pragmatic opportunity served to make possible a more genuinely shared social space. Most important, the ethos of the refugees extolled the value of all human beings and their basic equality before God; taken seriously—and the people of this community take their values very seriously—this meant that women were entitled to the same privileges and responsibilities as men.

Two middle-aged sisters discussed these changes in consciousness about women's roles. "Now women are as valuable as men," explained María S. "Before, they said that only men had value, that women didn't count for much. We lived in the kitchen. Now we've learned a lot of things. For example, the women who are in the front fight just like the men, so they have to raise their level. Us too, even though we're old, but at least we do what we can. Before, in various ways we felt oppressed. The man always had the money and the woman was submissive to him. Now that shouldn't exist, she shouldn't be submissive. Although love of women by men is natural, neither one nor the other should be submissive."

Opposite: Washing corn, the first step in the production of tortillas.

Her sister described how the ethical strength of this new attitude was rooted in liberation theology. "This changed through study, and the talks that were given. Before, around 1972, I took a year-long course that Miguel Ventura [a Salvadoran priest] gave [in the village] about women. . . . He spoke about these things, to give some clarification. In the camp, the changes in consciousness were more rapid. All those things that the priest taught us we only really understood there in the camp. I understood it there because I was suffering, because I had also suffered here. There we saw things that he had explained to us."

Social equality between men and women in Colomoncagua was most evident in public life, and public life centered around work. Most jobs were done equally by men and women, although some tended to be assumed largely by one or the other gender. At times this conformed to expected patterns: workers in sewing, knitting, and pottery-making workshops were mostly female, and generally it was men who made tools and musical instruments. But the sexual division of labor in the camp revealed considerable diversity as well. In the mechanics workshop, for example, where the refugees learned to service automobiles and machinery, about one-quarter of the trainees were women. And in the technical training school, women learned—and taught—administration, mechanical drawing, art, mathematics, and office skills alongside of men. It was not just at the level of the shop floor that sexual equality was apparent. Often the responsables were women, even when most of the workers were male. Thus, in a hammock-making workshop, the only female in sight was a young girl still in her teens; she was in charge of the facility, supervising men old enough to be her grandfather and boys as young as ten or eleven. "Is this a problem for you?" we asked her, and the reply was given with a smile: "No, no problem at all." Over and over, this was the response to the same question put to women who worked in nontraditional settings.

In the camp, women's roles expanded at the same time that new opportunities opened up for men. The form of social organization that had emerged there, as well as the assistance of international agencies with resources for training and production, allowed both men and women to develop skills and expertise that were never even considered before. No one was allowed to monopolize these gains. As one woman put it, "We think the thing that has enabled us to participate has been the collective life-style. That's made it possible for everyone who wishes to be able to work. Before, over there, the men felt that it wasn't right for women to work, that was only for men to do. But here we feel that everyone has a right to work at what they're interested in. We have the right to participate equally with men."

Another woman described the progress that women made in the camp in this way: "The men have learned that the women are capable of working, they've come to accept this. . . . They've recognized that there [in El Salvador] they had an unjust relationship with the woman, and over here, many of them have learned to live as *compañeros* [partners or mates] equally. Maybe they both work—the woman in one workshop, the man in another;

After the corn has been rough-ground in the mill, it is fine-ground by hand on a stone, in the same way that it has been done for millenia. Water and lime are added in this step.

they leave for work together, the children go to the *guardería* [nursery]. If he comes home first, he takes care of the children. Or at least in some cases, because a lot of women don't have compañeros."

Admitting to the struggles that this entailed, she continued: "There are some men who try to prevent their wives from working or developing work skills, or doing the work they want to do, but some of the women are learning from this situation and have broader criteria than the husband does and don't accept the husband not letting them work. The women are doing it even if the men don't want them to."

Where the division of labor in the camp was sex-segregated, it came about because of preference or long-standing tradition rather than restrictions or active pressure. For example, the labor-intensive work of making tortillas, traditionally done by women alone at home, in the camp involved both men and women, but not equally in all stages of the production process. Both worked together at the laborious task of washing and grinding the corn, lifting the huge tin buckets heavy with kernels soaking in water, and operating the crude electric mill to produce the corn flour. But in the smoke-filled collective kitchens, where the *masa* (dough) was ground by hand on grinding stones and then slapped into shape and set onto the flat *comales* to cook, only women worked. Apparently a few men had tried to do this job, but everybody agreed that they were too slow. In the new settlement, however, boys as well as girls are apprenticed to this workplace, so the next generation may eradicate this vestige of sex segregation altogether.

The very fact that tortilla production had become a work area in the camp—and the collective kitchen was a workshop like any other—illustrates the community's commitment to improving the situation of women. In rural El Salvador, making tortillas—each woman isolated in her own home—is a major part of the day's responsibilities for women, along with caring for the children, preparing meals, and tending to the garden and livestock. While in urban areas many Salvadoran women have made great strides, in the *campo* (countryside) women's lives are still restricted to serving their husbands and families, performing labor that is both privatized and devalued. In Colomoncagua, this had changed, not just by pronouncements about women's equality, but more concretely by socializing women's work and thereby making it the responsibility of the whole community. In this way, the community showed that it valued women's work, making it visible as real labor and affording it the same legitimacy as other production and service activities. Indeed, the particularly harsh conditions of working in the collective kitchens (especially the constant smoke) were acknowledged by having substitute workers take over on Saturdays, giving the regular staff a shorter work week and still ensuring that fresh tortillas were available six days a week.

The establishment of *guarderías,* day-care centers for infants and toddlers, was another part of the deliberate strategy to free women for more varied social roles in the camp. These were set up by the Committee of Mothers, a part of the pastoral structure; few men participated in the actual running of the centers, although many men assumed childcare duties with older children, as children's coordinators. In this way, children became the responsibility of the community as a whole, not just of mothers or individual families. Work leaves were available so that mothers (and, presumably, fathers as well) could take care of sick youngsters. And the ease with which children were casually integrated into life in general in the camp undoubtedly went a long way toward making women's full participation possible. It was no problem to nurse an infant during a meeting or stop in to visit a toddler in the guardería during a work break. In some workshops, children would wander by and visit with their parents while they were working. Since the workplace and home were typically in close proximity in the camp, the boundaries between one's role as parent and worker were permeable and flexible.

Making furniture in the carpintería workshop.

This is not to suggest that full sexual equality had been achieved in Colomoncagua, nor to assume that the eradication of gender distinctions altogether was the refugees' goal. In many ways, the community sorted itself out on the basis of gender. This was apparent with children, whose informal play was typically sex segregated. Boys and girls played mostly in same-sex groups, often with very different kinds of games: younger boys rode down the hills on little wooden carts, while older boys (and men) played cards or came together in a lively game of tag similar to the ring-a-levio of our childhood. Girls played a form of jacks, with pebbles substituting for the metal pieces (and usually even for the ball). Sometimes they played tag too, but in their own energetic groups, separate from the boys. Organized sports were different for boys and girls as well, with boys and men playing soccer and girls and women playing European handball—a vigorous soccerlike game using a thrown, instead of kicked, ball—and, toward the end of their stay in the camp, a spirited version of softball.

Clothing for males and females was generally distinct. Women and girls almost always wore skirts or dresses, the typical clothing of women throughout Central America, especially in the countryside. Many women in the camp said they wanted to wear pants, but when they did the Honduran

Distributing pig skin and fat to the families.

soldiers accused them of being guerrillas, and so the community generally discouraged it. Some women who worked in traditionally male areas did, however, regularly wear pants. And the sturdy work boots the refugees learned to make in the camp were worn by women as well as men, topped by the distinctive striped socks knitted in the camp. Often, though, women seemed to prefer the convenient rubber sandals used throughout Central America.

Despite the enormous strides made by women in the camp, in the viviendas more traditional relationships persisted. Women in the home still assumed responsibility for preparing food, cleaning up, washing clothes, and caring for the children. Men may have helped out—playing with the kids

Opposite: When UNHCR cut off the feed for the pigs in August 1989, the refugees began to slaughter them while they were still fat. Here, newly butchered pigs are being further divided to be distributed to the families.

while the mother was cooking, occasionally washing a dish or wiping a child's bottom—but their role in domestic tasks was usually secondary. This inequity was not as significant as it may seem, given that so much of life in the camp took place in the public realm. Little time was spent indoors, or separately as a family unit, so there just wasn't that much to do in the home. Meals were simple and casual—grabbing a bowl of stew or a tortilla wrapped around some filling, and eating on the doorstep or in a hammock. And straightening up is not much of a chore when there are so few possessions to bother with: no table to set or furniture to polish, no stacks of dishes mounting in the sink.

But while gender division in private life remained apparent in the camp and was an issue for at least some women, other concerns took priority. The women in the community have a long-range view of change that gives them confidence that a new society is being constructed, despite pockets of resistance. As one woman put it, "The men still think that they're not capable of learning how to cook or take care of the house, but here the kids are learning that if they want to eat, they cook. If they come to the house and they're hungry, they find an egg or they get some food; they can't depend on their mother to do it for them. In that sense the kids are learning."

It should come as no surprise that there has been greater progress toward gender equality in this community in public life than in private, as this has been the experience of women around the world, in all countries, rich and poor alike. Increased opportunities for women in the workplace are typically not matched by egalitarianism in the home; women complain the world over of their double load. And it should be remembered that few women in poor nations enjoy entitlement to formal public equality as do the women of this community.

Moreover, the gender distinctions described here do not imply a generalized hierarchy of power and status in the community. In fact, decision making and leadership in the camp was remarkably well balanced sexually. Women and men served in almost equal numbers on leadership bodies and committees of all kinds and at all levels, and women's participation was far from token or behind-the-scenes. Since women greatly outnumbered men in the community, equal representation may not at first seem that significant. However, given the background of these people—and the reality that in similar situations, men often continue to dominate, even as a minority—we find important symbolic meaning in equal representation. And these women in fact exercised real leadership. At small and large meetings alike they played a strong and visible role, speaking out publicly and actively guiding the process. The slow, hesitant manner of the refugees, reflecting their campesino origins, undoubtedly opened space for women to speak and participate—in sharp contrast to the quick, aggressive style often required to participate in meetings in the United States.

The *bienvenidas,* welcoming gatherings for foreign visitors, involving music and speeches by members of the community and guests, were regularly chaired by women, so that their forceful role in the community was apparent to outsiders right away. When the refugees staged a massive confrontation with officials from UNHCR to challenge cutbacks in support, women's voices were heard along with men's, shouting out questions and challenges. It was a woman who, in November 1989, took charge of the first repatriation, leading a group of seven hundred refugees on a march back to El Salvador in a bold move taken without formal permission from the Salvadoran or Honduran authorities. Before, all this would have been impossible; after the experiences in Colomoncagua, it had become natural.

The women had come to Colomoncagua as typical Salvadoran campesinas, confined and subservient because they were women. They left as compañeras, partners in a new, shared existence, impatient to begin their new lives in El Salvador.

RELIGION

> "Before we came here, I used to pray the Rosary. I thought God was in heaven and would reward me when I died. Now I think that God is in the community."

Like most Salvadorans, the refugee community is almost entirely Catholic, and religion has great meaning for many of them. In El Salvador, it was nuns and priests and even an archbishop who took up their cause and were martyred in their name. The Catholic church gave their plea for social justice respectability and offered them what protection and solace it could.

But this was not the same church of their parents and grandparents, which traditionally had allied itself with elites and disregarded the poor. This was a new Catholicism born out of liberation theology, the reform movement that swept through Latin America in the 1970s and 1980s. Drawing from the theologians Leonardo Boff of Brazil and Gustavo Gutiérrez of Peru, fueled by the liberalizing policies of the Second Vatican Council in 1962, and confirmed by the conference of Latin American bishops in Medellín, Colombia, in 1968 and Puebla, Mexico, in 1979, liberation theology asserts that the church must side with the poor and concern itself with earthly matters such as injustice and oppression. Going back to early Christian practice and teaching, this radical theology emphasizes the equality of all people before God and the sanctity of human community. The hierarchical nature of traditional Catholicism is rejected in favor of a more democratic vision of a community of worshipers.

Spreading like wildfire among the poor in many regions of Latin America, liberation theology has been extremely popular in El Salvador. Christian base communities, groups of worshippers with lay leaders who provided religious instruction rooted in dialogue and discussion rather than doctrine and ritual, became a common focus for community organizing in the countryside and in the cities. In these groups, people discussed the meaning of the Bible as it related to their own lives, and found in it inspiration for their suffering and hope for a new and more just society. Often, these communities were not only structures for worship and spiritual reflection, but also vehicles for building cohesive communities and mobilizing people for action. Liberation theology represents a radical egalitarianism in religious practice and in social and economic life; its acceptance implies changing one's focus from personal salvation to community liberation.

In a very real sense, the community that was developed by the refugees in Colomoncagua represented the incarnation of the values of liberation theology. Here people lived together in harmony and equality, sharing what little they had to ensure that everyone's needs were met, encouraging each one's participation, and valuing each one's concerns. Their community was a secular one, however. Religious ideology clearly provided inspiration and guidance and was a source of sustenance for the refugees, but the social structures they created were not theological in nature. Governance was separate from spiritual practice; religious references and vocabulary were part of the everyday speech of only some members of the community. There was an active core of religious organizers and people who attended mass regularly, but there was also a large group who professed Catholicism but were not involved in church activities. A small minority were Protestants and a handful were nonbelievers. But all these groups drew a social and human inspiration from liberation theology, and they all worked together in harmony.

The spiritual needs of the community were met in several ways. Formal worship, including masses, was provided by the camp priest, beginning with Father Miguel, a Spaniard, who served for several years and was replaced in 1985 by Father Dennis, a Jesuit from New York City. Three grass-roots groups of refugees worked with the priest and provided their own religious leadership: first, the Delegates of the Word, lay catechists (male and female) who assisted in mass, gave convocations in Father Dennis's absence, and led discussions of Scripture. Then there were the Congregation of Christian Men for Peace, an organization set up in 1987 by Father Dennis for men who had "committed themselves to a Christian life in word and deed," and the Committee of Mothers, an equivalent women's organization which, among other things, ran the guarderías and looked out for the interests of the more than two hundred orphans in the refuge, whom they placed with refugee families. In addition, children were given regular lessons in catechism as a part of the activities organized by the children's coordinators.

"We came together originally as strangers," a member of the Congregation of Christian Men for Peace explained, speaking of both his group and the refugee community more generally.

> In our country we were Catholic but we didn't have the opportunity to understand what that religion means. The priests gave us mass and prayer, but we never really understood anything about the Bible; we couldn't take it up and read it to analyze how God wants us to live in the world. In the mass, the priests were the

A Sunday mass.

only ones to speak, and they spoke in other languages. We didn't know the principles of what God wanted. Here in exile, we've been able to make the Bible more clear, according to our discussions. For this reason, we feel more content, we feel a love for one another, and we come together as brothers.

Another member of the Congregation joined in: "Here we've been able to grow. In our organizations we have the opportunity to make proposals, among ourselves and toward countries that are in solidarity with us. We've opened roads of communication. Priests have visited here, and they've taken these experiences from us with them. When we lived in El Salvador we talked about the church, but we didn't practice it—everything was individual, nothing in community. Here it's been different. We dream that we'll go on being the same when we return."

The Congregation's weekly meetings in each subcamp combined Bible study with broader political education, analyzing pamphlets, for example, about Central American history or human rights. The leader would read a passage aloud, and then would encourage a discussion of the meaning of what was read. For them, this was how they "celebrated" their work. Their

A meeting of the Delegates of the Word, lay religious activists.

discussions focused on such themes as the dangers of greed, United States domination of the hemisphere, and the ways in which poor people were exploited and taken advantage of by the wealthy. When the Bible was read, the men would stand respectfully, and at various times in the meeting, the congregation would stand and sing hymns together. Once a month, leaders from each subcamp congregation would all come together to plan their activities.

The Delegates of the Word had a similar approach to their work, although this group was composed of both men and women and provided broader religious leadership for the community, working alongside of or in the absence of the clergy. The Delegates were also organized on the subcamp level, with leaders from all the subcamps coming together regularly for their own instruction and planning.

▲   ▲   ▲

One August Sunday the morning meeting of the Delegates from the whole refuge has a special guest: Father Dennis has been joined by a Jesuit priest

A meeting of the Delegates of the Word, lay religious activists.

from El Salvador, Father Segundo Montes, an occasional visitor to the camp and well loved by the refugees. The session is run like a seminar: the sixty or so men and women sit with notebooks in their laps, listening to the two priests give an informal presentation, after which they break down into smaller groups for discussion. Before they begin, an agenda is written on the blackboard and a head count is taken so enough lunch can be prepared. The atmosphere is serious and subdued, and yet relaxed and welcoming.

The focus for the meeting is the Fifth Commandment: Thou shalt not kill. Passages from Exodus are read to show the contradiction between the stark prohibition against killing given to Moses and the frequent transgression of that prohibition, apparently with God's approval. "What does this mean?" Father Dennis asks. "How is it that sometimes the Bible says that it's necessary to take a human life?"

A North American woman, a social worker who works in the camp as a Jesuit volunteer, explains that this issue is a painful one for the community because many of the refugees have not only experienced killing but have participated in it, as combatants in the war. They feel a deep crisis of conscience, which Father Dennis is trying to heal.

Segundo Montes rises to speak, his tall frame, gray hair, and deep voice giving him special authority. "The fundamental principle is not to kill," he agrees. "But there are many ways of killing. To prevent people from getting medicine or food is to kill. A boss who pays his workers too little to make more money for himself is killing his workers. The rule throughout the Bible is that whoever kills for selfish reasons is a sinner. People who kill out of self-interest, to maintain their power, are wrong."

The Delegates listen carefully, some nodding, as Father Segundo continues. "When someone kills in solidarity with those who have suffered, the Old Testament always defends this, when there's no other way. Even the Constitution of El Salvador of 1952 says that people have the right to rebel. Life is the most important thing. If all peaceful struggle hasn't helped, then taking up arms is to defend life. Self-defense is always recognized as just, even if it means that someone dies. This is the contradiction that appears in the Bible."

Father Dennis asks the group to react, to give their views. Several questions are raised, about the correctness of the death penalty, about the motives of the disciple who betrayed Jesus, about the reasons why the church in El Salvador is divided. "Isn't it true," says one man, "that the bishops aren't in favor of the poor? How can that be, don't they study the same Bible?" Father Dennis answers by reminding them that not everybody has the same point of view: "The person who doesn't hear the clamor of the poor can't understand the laws of God." Father Segundo points out that some church leaders are afraid:

> They see what happened to Archbishop Romero. Others don't want their power taken away. They've forgotten their purposes. The same thing happened in the temples in the Bible—the priests ended up defending the temple, forgetting the people. Because they live with the privileged, they forget the poor. There are others who haven't overcome the notion that everything that is Marxism is bad. The leaders of the guerrillas are Marxists and Christians too, but they can't accept that. They view them with suspicion, as a threat to the church. It's not true, but it's like they have cataracts; it clouds their vision.

"Some of the church leaders may have had humble origins," Montes continues, "but they've become privileged, like military officers. I hope the same thing doesn't happen to you," he teases, "because it happens. Union leaders, for example, get a better position, they want to go to the United States, they forget their roots. It happens, with government leaders, with priests. That's the way we are."

There is a general discussion of the moral complexities that result from men being forcibly drafted into the Salvadoran army and made to kill. The group agrees that God understands the draftees better than their superiors, who have a choice. And on the other side, someone points out, people may fight for bad reasons; maybe they join the guerrillas just because they want to kill soldiers, and will kill them when they could capture them.

After a five-minute break, the assembly counts off so that they can form smaller discussion groups. This format, with its emphasis on exchanging ideas, was unknown to most of the refugees before they came to Colomon-cagua. They were used to listening and following instructions, not making decisions for themselves. They're still in the process of learning to participate, and must practice speaking loudly enough so that others can hear. In the small groups, the discussions start off hesitatingly, but then flow more smoothly. In earnest tones they talk about the suffering their people had to endure, especially from poverty, and how this represented a kind of violence that they were justified in rising up against. Some take notes, so that they can report back to the larger meeting. After about forty-five minutes, the small groups come together in plenary session, each giving a summary of the points that were raised. Then it's time for a lunch break, and the Delegates line up to wash their hands and then walk to the nutrition center for their shared meal.

▲   ▲   ▲

During mass, hundreds of people crowd into one of the four simple buildings that serve as chapels in the camp, some sitting on crude benches, others standing. There were two masses every Sunday, rotating around the refuge, as well as on Christmas, New Year's, and other special days. From the ceiling, decorative bits of cut colored paper are hung, giving the place a festive air. Women are in the majority here, many of them older, their heads covered with a small kerchief or cloth. Babies are held and nursed when they cry, and small children watch with wide-eyed attention. There is a good deal of music in this ceremony; the camp *conjunto* (band) plays, the violin singing along with the voices of the children's chorus. The Bible verses are read by Delegates and other members of the community. Some are newly literate and read with effort. Everyone listens patiently and nods support. The communion wafers are distributed by Delegates who pass through the crowd. If Father Dennis can't be present to say mass, the refugees conduct their own Celebration of the Word, led by the Delegates and almost the same as mass but without the communion.

The communal feeling is strong, and becomes even more intense when the song "Da Me La Mano" (Give me your hand) is sung and everybody extends the "hand of love" to those around them. Their voices are sharp and strong:

> It doesn't matter what race you may be
> Poor or rich, Christ calls you,
> If your heart is like mine,
> Give me your hand and we'll be brothers.

CHILDREN

"Look at the kids—they don't fight. They've learned how to live. We have an environment here that encourages them to live like brothers."

It was the children that visitors to Colomoncagua would notice first. Mobs of curious kids would follow them about, some shyly from a distance, giggling and running when noticed, others more boldly, offering a hand to shake or proudly showing that they had learned the name of the visitor: "Esteban! Hola!" Life seemed carefree, as children roamed about the camp, almost always in groups, playing and talking and laughing. They poked their heads into doorways and peered through windows, filled with curiosity, their eyes bright, breaking into broad smiles when someone paid attention to them. Sometimes they would become too intense and annoy the adults, who would shout at them or gesture threateningly, but rarely was there any real anger or blows. Generally the adults were extremely patient, gentle, and affectionate with them.

Children in the campo of El Salvador don't behave the same way, the refugees explained. There, children are more isolated from one another, usually having only their siblings or cousins as companions, and they are more shy, especially around strangers. Salvadoran children are usually quite timid and obedient with adults, fearing the harsh discipline of their fathers.

"We've learned to be different parents from our parents, who punished us a lot," said a middle-aged father of four, his second family. "Our kids are learning and we're learning how to teach them, so we're both learning. We used to use the strap a lot, but it's like we've learned in other areas: if you put people in jail, they come out worse. So we want to find a new way."

During their period of exile, the refugees were deliberate about finding this new way of childrearing. Children were no longer the responsibility of their parents alone; now the community had a stake in how they behaved and were treated. Day care was set up for infants and toddlers, and children's coordinators were chosen to organize and supervise older children's activities, so that women were effectively relieved of the burden of child care. As with so many areas of their lives, the refugees' method was to develop a common approach to managing children through discussions and meetings. Orientation sessions were held so that the hundred or so people who worked with kids in the camp could give suggestions to parents about how to handle them. Patience and gentle guidance were preferred over coercion and punishment.

A young mother explained: "In the past, everyone raised their own kids as best they could. But here, the kids are organized at a very young age. They talk about things, about life, about the new way of living, and organization—we never thought about things like that." Another young woman with three children described the effectiveness of the new methods: "We parents have a right to give advice to our children. At the same time the coordinators talk to the kids about not fighting, about discipline. Between the two, we've been able to end the fighting."

Her father attributed this achievement to the consistency of the guidance children received in the camp: "The teaching here is a unified thing. The instructors in the schools also teach them not to fight, to live here as brothers. The children's coordinator tells them the same thing, and the parents too. So there's a unity in all the messages they're getting. This is all part of what we call popular education. The parents are getting a new idea of how to deal with kids, not to punish them, to tell them what to do."

Every morning except Sunday, at about five o'clock, just as the roosters settled down from their predawn crowing, the children's coodinators in each neighborhood would walk among the dwellings, ringing a little bell to gather the children together for the morning's activities. There was a set schedule:

An early-morning sectoral meeting of the children in Limón II.

Salvadorans are crazy for soccer. These cipotes are playing with a homemade ball of rags and string.

two days a week it was catechism class, another two days, games and sports, and the other days, meetings. The activities lasted no more than an hour, before school or work. Attendance was voluntary and usually enthusiastically anticipated; it was the children's special time, a way to begin their day in community.

▲   ▲   ▲

In catechism class about sixty kids, ranging in age from four to ten or eleven, sit in a circle, listening to the leader who is reading and speaking from a notebook. "What's the correct path?" he asks in the recitation style of Catholic pedagogy. The leader provides the answers as well as the questions: "To live in fraternity and community, to really love each other. To follow the First Commandment means to love the people around you. What is justice? Justice is being with the community, not allowing bad things to happen, like war. What is injustice? Injustice is misery and ignorance and poverty and war."

The children sit half-listening, a bit restless, as if at school, sometimes giggling with each other, but the adults don't scold or insist that they be still. "I hope you're all listening," they are told. "Little by little you'll learn this. To learn doesn't mean just the words; we'll see if you'll live like this, everyday. . . . Because when we go back to our country and there will be children from Morazán, and they'll see the children from Colomoncagua, what kind of example will you be?" When the leader is finished, the children line up to count off so they know how many attended, and then they all march off to get a warm cup of milk (if available) or atol.

The adults seem untroubled by the restlessness and inattention, as if they know that the lessons will be repeated so often and in so many different contexts that they'll inevitably sink in. Their patience also stems from the acceptance of children as they really are, instead of imposing an artificial discipline or unrealistic expectations.

▲   ▲   ▲

The strong role played by the community in structuring the lives of children in the camp no doubt developed as a response to the potentially chaotic situation of such a large concentration of youngsters in a confined—and at times dangerous—space. Children outnumbered adults in the camp, as having many offspring was almost as common there as it had been back home. But they couldn't roam wherever they wanted because of the threat of patrols by Honduran soldiers, who had been known to attack and seize them. The densely populated living conditions in the camp, making private space virtually nonexistent, combined with the highly organized social life—where work, school, meetings, and other group activities filled the day for adults and children alike—meant that in some sense community life replaced family life. Not that family was unimportant—indeed, family ties were very strong for the refugees—but rather that children spent more time with their peers playing informally or in organized social activities in the camp than with their parents, and people generally spent more time in larger social groups than in family units.

In effect, then, the programs and structures for children became a means of socializing them to a communal life-style and building a collective consciousness. The refugees very deliberately accustomed their children at an early age to a social life that was rooted in collective discussion and action, and in so doing, took them seriously as members of the community. Children in Colomoncagua constituted a sector, a kind of demographically defined interest group, along with women, men, youth, and the war-disabled, that would meet regularly—and separately—to discuss its concerns. In this way, the community formally established children as a distinct constituency with its own needs, rights, and responsibilities. Although the children's meetings were mostly adult-directed, they provided young people with a concrete sense of their significance and purpose in community life.

▲   ▲   ▲

A 5:30 A.M. children's meeting is attended by about fifty kids, some as young as two or three, brought along by older brothers or sisters. They listen as the coordinator, a young man with the manner of a kindly camp counselor, talks about the importance of taking care of community property. Through gentle but persistent repetition the message is driven home. The specific issue is the damage caused by playing in newly planted areas, but the deeper concern is the children's role as members of the community.

> We have to take care of these plants, we can't go pulling them up or bothering them. Now how can we take care of them? With the help of everyone, right? It's not just the responsibility of the children's coordinator; I can't take care of the plants alone. This has to be done by everybody. Because here the children are part of the community, right? And since the whole community has helped to plant them, all of us have the right to take care of them. It's clear that if as children we start to take care of them, or of whatever we may have, then in the future we'll be better youth and adults who take care of things. And that tomorrow we'll teach this to the others.

He reassures the youngsters that their needs are important too. "We have to arrange a place where you can play, because we understand that play is a recreational thing. And that it keeps our spirits up. The important thing, I repeat, is to try to help one another. If there's a child who's doing something that's not good, disturbing the plants, you have to correct them, and not wait for a children's coordinator to be the one to come and correct them. Do you agree?" Here a few children respond: "Sí." He presses them further: "So, do you agree? It looks like only about four of you agree. Do you all agree?" Then they grin and shout with enthusiasm, "Sí!"

▲   ▲   ▲

The role of the children's coordinators involved more than leading meetings and organizing activities; they served as general caretakers for youngsters. If a child was hurt or upset, the coordinators would intervene, finding the child's parents if necessary. And they disciplined the children if they were troublesome, chasing them away from where they were doing mischief. Since life in the camp was quite loosely structured, with children,

Girls struggling over the ball in an improvised game of European handball.

even tiny ones, wandering about all the time, having these childcare workers on duty was a critical factor in ensuring a safe environment for children.

Most remarkably, one never saw the children of Colomoncagua fighting or playing war games. The significance of this fact should not be understated. This was a group of eighty-four hundred people, almost two-thirds of them children, who for nine years lived under cramped and impoverished circumstances, encircled by soldiers and haunted by memories of war. It would have been natural under such conditions to expect children to play war games and fight with one another, as the children of Northern Ireland or the Middle East—or rural El Salvador, for that matter—imitate the violence around them. But this didn't happen in Colomoncagua, a fact confirmed by our observations and by interviews with refugees and international staff who had lived in the camp for years.

One refugee leader explained that when they first came to the camp, the children started imitating the Honduran soldiers, and the refugees were disturbed by this. What could they do? As with so many issues in this community, they addressed the problem through discussions in neighborhoods, in the men's and women's groups, and in the children's meetings. Through a combination of gentle social pressure and strongly shared values, the community was able to guide its children away from violence.

Not that the children in Colomoncagua were angels. They were some-times restless and inattentive; the little ones would occasionally whine and fuss and quarrel like children anywhere. The kids could be intrusive at times, and some adults felt they needed greater discipline and control. But the children were clearly a welcome part of community life in the camp, fully integrated into the web of shared activities, tasks, and rewards. Children participated in workshops, attended meetings, and helped out in numerous ways: waiting in line to receive the allotment of meat for their families, unloading firewood from the trucks, distributing chickens (grabbed by the legs and proudly carried, upside down and squawking) to each household. They would even hold their own protest marches, carrying flags and banners to press for peaceful repatriation or an end to repression by the military.

A community meeting with representatives of the UNHCR in August 1989 in Copi-nol. The banner reads, Permanent Solution for the Refugees Is: To Repatriate as a Community.

Portrait made in the camp at Colomoncagua.

And the children took care of one another, exhibiting a tenderness and concern that was striking. A toddler would cry and an older child would comfort her; boys and girls alike would carry or watch over the littler ones. The adults set clear and consistent expectations for the children in the camp, provided direction and leadership, but then gave them a great deal of freedom to settle their own disputes, devise their own games, and find their own pleasures. And the kids responded well. For many of them, life in the refugee camp was their entire world. It was a world of privation and confinement, but also a world of mutuality, caring, and respect. They were the new citizens of a new society, a promised land.

OS LA ALTERNATIVA
PARA EL FUTURO
DE EL SLVAD

CROSSING BACK
RETURNING TO EL SALVADOR

▲▲

> Deep in our hearts, the desire to return always existed. The years passed and peace did not appear, and the moment arrived to decide to be participants in the construction of peace.

Until May of 1989, the refugees were determined to stay in the camp at Colomoncagua. For years they had resisted pressure from the Honduran government and military and UNHCR to relocate into the interior of Honduras, to move to other countries, or to repatriate. Their position was simple: they were refugees from the war; they wanted to return, but not until conditions in El Salvador made it possible to do that in peace and security. Also, leaving before the war ended and peace was stabilized would allow the Honduran military to claim the area as a military base, something they had long wanted to do. The militarization of the camp would complete a chain of bases along the border and would also eliminate the international presence the camp provided in the region. These developments would permit increased military cooperation between Honduras and El Salvador, and thus contribute to lengthening the war.

In the spring of 1989, the community's position changed. At the end of May, UNHCR sponsored the first International Conference on Central American Refugees (CIREFCA), held in Guatemala. Governments, nongovernment organizations, humanitarian agencies, and scholars were invited—but not refugees. Although they were not directly represented, the community at Colomoncagua sent a message in which they laid out a new position. Instead of renewing their call for international support for their determination not to return until the necessary conditions existed in El Salvador, they called for help in achieving those conditions. They began to talk publicly in this document about returning as a community to Morazán. This discussion released

Overleaf: A banner at the dedication celebration for Ciudad Segundo Montes: We Are the Alternative for the Future of El Salvador.

the desire to return, held in check by the refugees since December 1980, when the first people to arrive thought they were going to stay for a week or two, until things cooled down in their area.

RETURNING TO CANAAN

By August the community was determined to return, and projected the possibility of doing so by the end of the year; the idea of an imminent return had quickly become an overwhelming, dominant element of the consciousness of people throughout the camp, despite the bombs that could still be heard falling just over the border. Almost every conversation included some reference to the return, which usually evoked broad grins and enthusiastic nods. The mood was one of expectancy and optimism—and preparation for a difficult transition.

In January 1990 these two boys paused from play to look over the quebrada and the subcamps in the distance.

An outdoor mass in Limones, Christmas Day, 1989. When the camp was packing up for the move, the chapels were used as warehouses.

How are we to understand this profound and dramatic change in the community's position? "We can't be spectators any longer; we have to go back and be actors," explained one camp leader. Behind this apparently simple expression was a complex and increasingly urgent content, the result of various internal and external developments. Within the camp, the developments of the previous year—the consolidation of the new governance structure, a growing self-confidence based on numerous successes and accomplishments in the economic, social, and political areas, and an understanding that there was little more they could achieve until they were in a position to work toward economic self-sufficiency (which their situation in Honduras rendered impossible)—made the return seem an almost inevitable conclusion. The refugees felt that their next challenge was to transfer what they had accomplished in the harsh, but isolated and assisted, environment of the camp to the reality of Salvadoran peasant society and to participate in the national economy, social structure, and politics. They felt ready to bring back the work skills, the education, the political and administrative skills they had developed. By their own description, they had arrived as frightened, illiterate, backward, and miserable refugees; now they were prepared to return as trained, self-confident, experienced cooperators. They counted among their population literally hundreds of teachers, dozens of health paraprofessionals, scores of lay pastoral workers, and hundreds of skilled workers, mechanics, farmers trained in modern techniques, women experienced in political leadership, and so on. To take just one dramatic example of this change, their presence would raise the number of elementary-school teachers in northern Morazán from around twenty to over four hundred.

Furthermore, and perhaps more important in the long run, they would be bringing back all their experience in self-management and autonomous governance as well as a highly developed model of communitarian and collective life, which they believed to be directly applicable to the lives of their compatriots, especially the campesinos.

Externally, the election of the right-wing ARENA government in March 1989 presented a discouraging prospect that the war in El Salvador would go on for many more years. Paradoxically, that prospect contributed to the refugees' determination to return; the idea of waiting for peace to come began to mean waiting perhaps forever. The emergence of contradictions within ARENA; the development of a much broader, if not yet organizationally united, opposition movement in El Salvador; and the impulse of CIREFCA itself, which indicated international interest in movements toward repatriation, all added more direct and positive support to the idea of returning quickly. The summit conference of the Central American presidents in Tela, Honduras, in the first days of August was an important development for peace in the region and demonstrated the isolation and diplomatic weakness of the Cristiani government. The summit was read in the camp as an encouraging sign. Finally, recent moves toward negotiations between the government and the FMLN, however remote real progress may have seemed, added further impetus to the idea of returning.

The decision to go back was a declaration that the refugees were going to participate in the struggle to build a new El Salvador, both through their relationship with the remaining (greatly reduced) population of the zone of Meanguera and through the very attempt to reconstruct the social, political, and economic structures and activities they had developed in the camp. This was the meaning of "becoming actors."

Of course, the community recognized that returning would mean making some serious adjustments in their way of life. One major issue was that in El Salvador they would have to participate in the money economy, and this meant thinking about how workers were to be paid and how the community would be able to continue supplying the needs of those unable to work. One example of the ways they began to approach these problems is provided by a scheme they considered for managing egg production in their new settlements. In the camp, feed for the hens was provided by UNHCR until August

1989, when it was cut off. The eggs, like all food, were distributed on a per capita basis throughout the camp. Everyone, regardless of age, occupation (or lack of work), or position, received the same ration; the special needs of malnourished children, pregnant women, elderly people, and others were met through supplemental food provided by the nutrition centers. The henhouse workers, like everyone else in the camp, received no remuneration for their labor.

One plan under consideration for the new settlements in Morazán was to divide the egg production into thirds. One-third would go to the workers as their salary—presumably they would consume some of the eggs and sell the rest. One-third would be sold in the national or regional market to raise money for the purchase of feed and other needs and make the program economically self-sufficient. The final third would be distributed to young children, old people, and others who could not work.

This model raises an interesting issue. In order to sell its eggs, the new enterprise would need to have access to markets and to be able to bring in feed and other supplies. Both of these activities were very problematic because of military harassment of trucks carrying materials into and out of northern Morazán. One of the conditions the refugees successfully proposed to the government of El Salvador was that free transit and commerce with the rest of the country be guaranteed to the zone.

The refugees believed that returning would contribute to the development of Morazán, provide an impulse to the peace process, and in general allow them to rebuild a "real life." But in order for repatriation to have this meaning, it had to be a return of the entire community. In one sense, this is almost too obvious. What had been created was a community, not a set of individual improvements. The workshops and other social institutions they had created depended on people living and working collectively.

Also, the kinds of relationships and mutual support that were integral to the new sense of community required that people stay together. One of the accomplishments in Colomoncagua was a sense of common responsibility for all the members of the community. Thus, in an editorial, "Why Return As a Community?" in their newsletter, *La Esperanza* (Hope), the issue was raised:

> Very soon we are going to put ourselves in the framework of a country with a severe economic crisis aggravated by a nine-year-old war, . . . with a 40% unemployment rate, . . . with serious problems in the areas of health, education, housing, etc. So, what are the real prospects for subsistence for . . . the one thousand single mothers with approximately five children each, the five hundred old people, . . . many of whom have lost their family members because of repression or other causes, . . . and the orphans, 211 in number? . . . Because of all these things, the necessity of a repatriation as a community [comes] not only from the concrete advantages that this model for life offers people for

Children playing on the cement foundation of the already dismantled nutrition center of Limón I, December 1989.

resolving their problems, but also because in the current circumstances of the country, there is no space to resolve problems from an individual perspective. Especially when it's a case of a community like ours.

The residents of Colomoncagua therefore insisted on returning all at once, taking with them every house, workshop, shed; every tool and piece of machinery; their pigs and goats and chickens—in fact, everything they owned—in order to resettle in four places in the countryside near the village of Meanguera. Meanguera lies just north of the Torola River, the effective border between the part of northern Morazán under control of the FMLN and the rest of the department, under government control. It is an area that had been heavily bombed and largely depopulated, and most of the people in Colomoncagua came from there or nearby.

In August 1989, the first official delegation in nine years arrived in the camp from San Salvador. Although the delegation was there only to open contacts, and not for serious negotiating, the refugees were carefully optimistic about the contact. People in the camp expressed real joy at the possibility of returning, and some members of the government delegation seemed genuinely impressed with the accomplishments of the community (it is clear that the government had very little sense of what had been going on in the camp).

However, high Salvadoran military officials had already been pronouncing against the return, and especially against a return as a community. A week or so after the government visit to the camp, Salvadoran vice-president Francisco Merino announced that the refugees would be allowed to repatriate only in small groups, to be dispersed among the population or return strictly to their villages of origin. The refugees were characterized as a den of guerrillas and future guerrillas, an image promoted by the Honduran government and military and by the media in Honduras, El Salvador, and the United States.

On March 3, 1989, reporter Mark A. Uhlig (after spending only a couple of hours in the camp) wrote in the *New York Times,* in what was essentially a United States embassy brief, that Colomoncagua was a fearful, repressive

Loading galvanized roof panels onto one of the trucks carrying supplies to Meanguera, January 4, 1990.

place, an authoritarian society controlled by an FMLN-aligned clique. Similar distortions were heard on Spanish-language radio in Washington, D.C., and in some European newspapers, although all were publicly rejected by observers who visited the camp and agency personnel with more extended familiarity with the situation there. For the refugees, this was part of the long-term effort to discredit them and paint any opponents of the status quo in El Salvador as dangerous subversives or terrorists.

Meanwhile, in El Salvador, the issue of the return generated a great deal of interest. By July it was a regularly featured story in the Salvadoran media. By August, there already existed a support commission for the return, a coalition of Salvadoran grass-roots and nongovernment organizations. Shortly after the government delegation arrived in August, this commission also sent a delegation, consisting of members of the constituent organizations—the Christian Base Communities of El Salvador (CEBES), the Council for Community Development of El Salvador (PADECOES), the Salvadoran Foundation for Workers' Self-Management and Solidarity (FASTRAS), and the Lutheran World Federation—to discuss how to construct a supportive atmosphere and prepare the material conditions for the return.

In addition to planning and negotiating for their move, the refugees had to confront serious problems during the waiting period. The gravest of these was a deep and broad-ranging series of cuts in the budget of UNHCR, purportedly the consequence of a disastrous worldwide economic crisis the organization faced, with debts into the billions of dollars (for the eight years of the Reagan administration the United States did not pay its share, one-third of UNHCR's budget). The refugee leadership, acknowledging the problems UNHCR faced, still asked why such drastic cuts were announced just in the wake of the CIREFCA proposal. The announcement was felt by them as one more pressure to leave Honduras, no matter what the circumstances.

When the UNHCR administrator for western Honduras came to the camp in August, she explained in two open-air meetings—attended by hundreds of refugees—that the cuts would be only in the least urgent programs and would not touch nutrition or health. The crowds responded with skepticism, shouting out questions: "When the hens die from lack of food, will UNHCR bring us eggs?" "When the pigs die, will UNHCR bring us meat?" "When we run out of shoe leather, will you bring us shoes?" "If medicine hasn't been cut, why isn't there even an aspirin tablet in the health centers?"

Different explanations have been proposed for UNHCR's frequent conflicts with the refugees over the years. We do not find any particular one satisfying, but it does seem that UNHCR officials and many of the field staff were uncomfortable with the responsibility for these people, who were politically embarrassing, unwilling to play the role of docile and grateful recipients of aid, and insistent on developing their own path for their own future. The refugees wanted UNHCR to advocate on their behalf with the Honduran authorities; UNHCR saw itself more in a mediating role. What is certain is that the cuts in the budgets for the various workshop, sanitation, and farming programs were a serious threat to the refugees' ability to

Packing up half the subcamp of Copinol, January 9, 1990.

Dismantling houses, subcamp Copinol, January 9, 1990.

maintain their community in good health and morale in the short run, and to the level of success they could achieve in their resettlement in the long run.

In addition to negotiating the conditions of their return with the Salvadoran government, and their conditions of life with UNHCR for the period until then, the community had to arrange for the actual physical move. They had to take apart all the buildings—every vivienda, school, workshop, clinic, chapel, and latrine—in order to bring these with them to El Salvador. They had to pack up all their personal and communal goods: machinery, supplies, tools, furniture, educational and health materials, food stores, and so on. And, of course, they had to develop a structure for organizing this entire enterprise.

Finally, the route to Meanguera was an issue. They hoped to be able to take all their belongings in vehicles over a yet-to-be-completed road that ran directly to the area they wished to settle. If they had to return over existing roads, they faced a roundabout trip of several days through the interior of Honduras. So securing a promise from the Salvadoran government to complete the road was a high priority.

To many people's surprise, in discussions in September 1989 the Salvadoran government abandoned its opposition to the refugees' returning as a community to Meanguera. It also agreed to guarantee free transit and free commerce between Meanguera and the rest of the country. A government delegation was sent to the camp to provide temporary personal identification cards to the refugees, and a commitment was made to repair the dirt road linking Colomoncagua with Morazán. A schedule for returns, on trucks rented by UNHCR, was worked out, to be started in November.

Of course, a process of this magnitude required a great deal of organizational preparation, both for the move itself and to confront the new situation they would find in El Salvador. A set of commissions was established for Moving and Transportation, Economic Reactivation, Logistics, Health, Disassembly, and Reassembly, all responsible to the Comisión Coordinadora. Each consisted of four or five persons, who developed plans for their areas and organized work crews in the subcamps.

Preparation went beyond winning concessions in negotiations with government authorities and creating physical conditions for an efficient move. If the community was returning to El Salvador in order to extend further the social model they had developed in the camp, they would need a set of plans for life in their new settlement. This meant developing projects for economic reactivation and social organization. But it also meant creating a vision of what the community would look like physically.

To develop this vision, the community enlisted the help of architects and planners from Europe. From their consultations a scheme for a new town emerged, complete with ideas for constructing houses in stages to end up with modern and ecologically sound dwellings, with water provided to each home and every household connected to a sewer system. The new town was laid out with space reserved for schools, clinics, chapels, community buildings, warehouses, workshops, recreational areas, community gardens, and family plots for houses and gardens. The plan involved the creation of four hexagonal centers of about two thousand people each. These urban modules were designed to allow for expansion and ultimate connection with each other. To ensure safety and tranquility, traffic would be kept mostly on the periphery by locating production facilities there and saving the middle for schools, chapels, and parks.

Nothing of this kind has ever been seen in rural Central America; indeed, the long-term realization of these plans would place the new settlements in the forefront of rural community development in the entire world.

▲   ▲   ▲

The agreed-upon process was underway (although the community complained that the documentation and roadwork were going much slower than promised) when the FMLN offensive began throughout El Salvador on November 11, taking the government, the international community, and the refugees by surprise by its audacity and vigor. In response, the government recalled its delegation to the camp and suspended the repatriation process indefinitely.

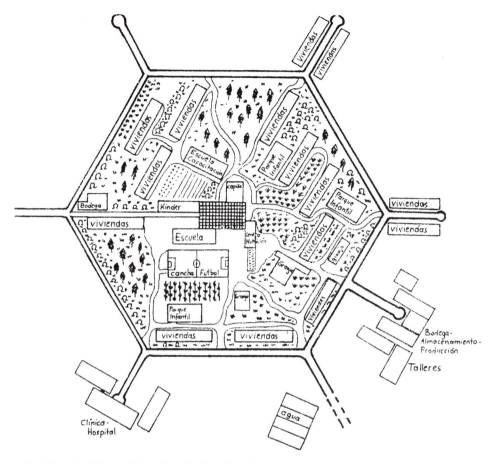

Architect's Original Plan for the New Settlements

This was a crisis for the community. Faced with an eager and impatient population on the one hand—by now a great deal of progress had been made in disassembling workshops and people were without work, waiting for the move—and government intransigence on the other, the leadership of the camp decided to act. Organized clandestinely, a small work crew of one hundred people from each of the two zones of Colomoncagua would leave for Meanguera on foot in order to begin work on some minimal physical infrastructure (essentially temporary latrines, warehouses, and road repairs). The plan was kept secret to avoid obstacles, since the group would go without permission from either the Salvadoran or Honduran government, and therefore without help from UNHCR. Despite the lack of official support and the uncertainties, many more than two hundred people wanted to go, and the leadership agreed to include another five hundred, provided they were all able to work in the construction of the new settlements.

Santos, whose husband, a man in his sixties, was one of the volunteers, took a break from chores with their daughters. They sat in their vivienda, describing the process and the motivation behind this first repatriation:

Gloria, a fourteen-year-old daughter, with four years' experience as a teacher: "First, there were a lot of meetings to discuss it and to choose the people who would go by work areas, three from each area of work. They were hoping they'd have vehicles that would carry food for them, but UNHCR didn't provide vehicles, so they decided to go on foot. Only these two hundred were going to go, but when they saw there were so many people who wanted to go, they decided to have volunteers.

"So in the end, all these people were really happy that they were going. The way my father decided to go was, seeing the people get ready to go, he said that he just couldn't stay here any more."

Santos, fifty-nine years old: "My husband told me that he was going to go in the first group. He said, 'I'm going there to work, because here there's no work, but there I'm going to work. And I'll be waiting for you there, and hopefully we will have developed things when you arrive.' He said that I should feel good, encouraged, waiting to get there."

"And how do you feel?"

The trucks with repatriating refugees roll out of Copinol, January 14, 1990.

Remounting the trucks to leave the camp.

"One feels good, because you know that he's happy, that he's gone to work. Of course, one gets sad, but at the same time I want to say that it gives you spirit when you see him go and he's so happy. And that we're going to get there also."

Sylvia, a nineteen-year-old daughter: "Most of the people are feeling very enthused about the fact that they're over there. And we're happy to know that he's there and that he's doing something [for] when we arrive . . . and so we feel full of spirit. We have the faith that all of us are going to get there soon, because with this trip, this first departure that those people made, we were able to see that we're also going to leave."

The unauthorized repatriation on November 18 was a joyous event, resonant with deep meaning for the refugees. An international observer describes the scene:

> Women, children, old folks, and men filled the road . . . to the tranca of the camp, loaded with as many possessions as they could carry. The march through the camp was filled with chants, shouts of "Que viva!" tears and applause from those staying behind. International visitors joined in and everybody headed to the tranca.
>
> As the refugees approached the military gate, the crowd was halted by a large number of armed Honduran soldiers. . . . The local Honduran lieutenant initially took the position that no one would be allowed to leave. In the face of the refugees' determina-

tion and with the intercession of the United Nations, however, he finally agreed to let them go—but made it clear that once they left, they would not be allowed back again. . . .

As we marched down the road into town, we could see hundreds of folks in the camp, cheering and waving us on. The border with El Salvador is some four kilometers from the town of Colomoncagua, and the returning refugees wasted no time in pushing through the village and out the other side. The day was turning very hot, and the group finally stopped to rest after one very long climb. People had come with everything they didn't want to leave behind—women carried huge loads of clothing, pots, and dishes on their heads; men held shovels, tools, even guitars in their hands while lifting great bundles on their shoulders;

The caravan of trucks leaves the camp at Colomoncagua bound for Meanguera, January 14, 1990.

Looking for personal possessions the day after arriving in Meanguera.

even the children came with improvised knapsacks on their backs and both hands filled—with chickens, a radio, a cherished notebook or box of goods. . . .

The repatriation had not been officially sanctioned, and everyone knew that the refugees were running a great risk in pressing their right to return to their homeland without approval. . . . As a result, the march was a tense one; in their effort to get to the border quickly, there was no time for the adults to rejoice in being free once again, or for the children to look around at a world they were seeing for the first time—adobe houses, lush flowers, a church, a village plaza, a schoolhouse on the road. Fearing that the Honduran military might try to seal the border to prevent their departure, the woman who led the repatriation kept the rest to a minimum, walking through the group to keep people's energies and enthusiasm high.

The repatriated refugees were joyously welcomed by family and friends in Morazán, and traveled over the next two days through Perquín and Jocoaitique on their way to Meanguera. Tragically, they were attacked by mortar fire from the Salvadoran army on November 29, and four of the community were seriously injured, including a seven-year-old boy and an eighteen-month-old girl. A report from PADECOMSM (The Council for Community Development of Morazán and San Miguel) stated that the attack was directed by Colonel René Emilio Ponce, chief of the Salvadoran high command, who had apparently accused the group of being armed by the FMLN. But even this violence failed to deter the refugees at Colomoncagua in their efforts to continue with their repatriation.

Based on the success of the November 18 departure and because of its own long-standing eagerness to see the refugees leave, the Honduran government cooperated in the planning for the next departure, on December 9. CONARE rented twenty-seven trucks to transport the people of La Esperanza subcamp and their possessions. For the community, this was their first chance to move an entire group of people—families, their possessions, the

Building a warehouse, Los Hatos, January 15, 1990. Warehouses, along with latrines and roads, are the most fundamental infrastructure and must be built immediately.

materials of their disassembled houses and buildings, and so forth. Because the Salvadoran government still was not cooperating (indeed, the government had characterized the November 18 repatriation as an "invasion"), the trucks would go only to the border crossing at Las Flores. Since the repatriation did not have the approval of the Salvadoran government, UNHCR was unable to help in any substantial way or to provide the financial benefit normally given to repatriating refugees and promised to this community. But when the trucks arrived to unload at the border, the refugees on board found many people from the first group and residents of the area waiting to help them, along with a few vehicles to move their possessions further along.

The repatriations of November and December were important events for the community. In the first place, they were tests of their organizational preparations, their ability to administer the departures, and their social discipline. The results were encouraging; even as they learned a great deal during the course of each departure, they were more convinced than ever of their ability to undertake such a move.

The departures were also important for morale in the community. They demonstrated both the seriousness of the commitment to return and that the return was going to happen soon. They also demonstrated the community's ability to confront setbacks successfully. Finally, they provided sorely needed work and activity—nothing seems to hurt the morale of this group of people as much as idleness.

The community was clearly ready. As the year drew towards its end, the big question was whether the authorities were also ready.

▲   ▲   ▲

In mid-December, discussions began to get the repatriation process back on track. Representatives from CONARE, UNHCR, and the government of El Salvador worked out a plan to resume repatriating the community from Colomoncagua to Meanguera, beginning on January 14, 1990. Under this plan, the UN would contract the services of one hundred trucks to transport the community with their personal and collective goods in groups of about five hundred people every four days. The plan also included repatriating the refugee community from the nearby camp at San Antonio, although their destination was not decided until much later (in the end, the Salvadoran government agreed to allow them, too, to settle where they wanted to, in Gualcho, Usulatán).

On December 22, a tripartite delegation from the parties described above went to the camp and met with the refugee leadership, who accepted the proposal in principle. The agreement produced a cautious optimism in the community, despite skepticism about whether the government would live up to its commitments.

For a couple of days before Christmas, a strong *norte*, the dry, cold north wind, blew through the camp, producing coughs and cracked lips and keep-

Feeding work crews who are clearing land, unloading trucks, and building a warehouse in Los Hatos, Meanguera, January 14, 1990.

ing people huddled in *viviendas* and other buildings at night. But the cold could not contain the enthusiasm for the season and the impending move. "Los cuchos! Los cuchos!" (the pigs, the pigs) the kids screamed with delight as a truckload of pigs, donated by the agencies, was brought in to be slaughtered to make *nacatamales*, the seasonal variety of the *tamal*, a food made from corn masa filled with various vegetables or meat, wrapped in banana leaves, and boiled. Agencies and foreign visitors brought flour and sugar, and a variety of breads was made in the camp. Finally, on Christmas Eve, there was a dance and a midnight mass, held under the stars and exposed to a strong wind of nearly freezing temperatures. All the celebrations were imbued with the momentous quality that this would be the last Christmas in Colomoncagua.

Christmas Day was a regular work day for most people; it was marred by the bombs, which could be heard falling over the very areas to which the

One of the champas in El Quebrachal where the repatriated families live, waiting for the provisional houses to be built.

community was going to return. "This violates the holiday cease fire," one man said. "It's a message to us." And the message was clear: the Salvadoran government would continue to bomb areas of civilian population, and returning to Morazán could be dangerous. But the determination to return was unshaken. One refugee, a forty-eight-year-old man who had learned to read and become a math teacher in the camp, accompanied a visitor up the winding path from the quebrada, offered some boiled water from the covered container in his vivienda, and said:

> We know that the country is at war, and that we might suffer, but we're suffering equally here. Because here we're in jail, we could say that, because we can't leave to go anywhere. And we have repression by the authorities, the soldiers. We could say we're encircled. To have left from there because of repression and to be here with the same repression, and sometimes there isn't enough

food to fill one. . . . So we've all decided that it's better to leave as a community for Meanguera, and there to see how we'll live. . . . Of course we're afraid of [the bombing], but you become brave out of fear itself. . . . If we die, we'll die in our own country. And that's what we want. Because I don't want to die in some other place, fleeing.

By New Year's Day the weather calmed, and the celebration was bigger and more joyous as the refugees felt the nearness of repatriation.

On January 4, under the terms of the agreement, a small group of five trucks was supposed to arrive to load up with building supplies and materials, tools, and food to be sent to the people who had left for Meanguera in the first two departures. As the date approached, it was seen in the community as a test of the commitment and good will of the two governments and UNHCR.

At about four o'clock, well before sunup, the trucks arrived at the traffic control booth the refugees had erected at the entrance to the camp. They were greeted by refugees responsible for transportation and loading, who directed them to the various spots where the materials were to be put aboard.

One of the trucks needed repairs to a front spring, and the welding was done in the mechanical workshop. This delayed the departure of the group for some time, but was another reminder of the community's ability to handle problems they might encounter in the process.

Finally, toward midmorning, the trucks left. Loaded with cement, lumber, roofing panels, nails, tools, dried corn, rice, and beans, and carrying a repatriating refugee in the cab of each vehicle next to the Honduran driver, they passed through a noisy, jubilant send-off by the community.

The next day, when some journalists who had accompanied the trucks returned to the camp, they brought back an open letter from the twelve hundred repatriated members of the community. It was addressed to their international supporters, but the mimeographed copies were read eagerly by the refugees:

> We have been well received by the communities of northern Morazán, . . . who have given us food and lately have been giving it to us on credit; they have to because they only produce corn and they sell it to cover their basic necessities.
>
> . . . We have picked four lots of coffee in Perquín; four warehouses and sixty-nine huts of plastic and branches have been built; the repairs to the road from San Fernando to the border are finished. We can see that the conditions exist to live in Morazán; there is a great hope on the part of the communities of Morazán that our arrival will be the window for their development. The problem that we have is that the Military Detachment No. 4 [the government military authority in the zone] will not give permission to enter to any institution. This is something we need, in

More champas in El Quebrachal.

order to be able to explain our urgent necessities to them, such as food, medicine, installing a water system, building and repairing more roads, transportation, building more huts, and other things, since we do not have sufficient funds to pay for them.

With respect to our security, we haven't had any incidents on the part of either of the armed groups [the government army or the FMLN] except for the 25th of December, when two A-37 airplanes bombed in the outlying areas of Perquín and Jocoaitique.

The shipment of the supplies and the enthusiastic communication from the people already in Meanguera provided another important moment in the preparations for the massive repatriation to come. All the powers and institutions that the refugees had to rely on had carried out their agreements. Morale went up another visible step, and preparations began for disassembling the houses of the five hundred people who would be next to leave, about one-half of the subcamp Copinol, in ten days.

During that week and a half, the pace of preparatory work stepped up. The construction crew worked on the model of the provisional houses proposed for construction in the new settlements, making changes in the original plans and soliciting comments from the community. The Salvadoran immigration delegation arrived on January 8 and began to produce identity cards. The leadership was in consultation with the Honduran authorities and UNHCR, working out the details of the departures. Plans were made for hospitality for the expected guests, diplomats, and journalists. The Asamblea de Comités met to consider a new political structure for the settlement.

The leadership developed a proposal to the community about a potentially delicate matter: the roughly twelve hundred people who had left on the first two repatriations had not received the cash benefit—the equivalent of fifty dollars—for repatriating refugees offered to each adult by UNHCR (children were to get half that amount). Although a small sum, it was more cash than most of the refugees had ever seen at one time. The proposal was for those who would now be leaving to share their benefit with those who had gone before. The idea was discussed in subcamp assemblies. Although it met with wide approval, there were some who objected:

"This money belongs to my family, so they can have more resources to get started again in Morazán. I don't intend to share it with anyone."

"But the people who went ahead have been working all this time for all of us. Because they went ahead to do this work, they didn't get the benefit. I think it is very important that we show them our support, and share what we have."

"Everything we have accomplished in this camp has been because of our unity. Our unity is the most important thing we have. I think we have to show unity with those who are in Meanguera now, and give them some of what we get."

Collective kitchen under the trees, Los Hatos I, March 1990.

The discussion went on until everyone who wanted to speak had his or her say. Then there was a vote. It was overwhelmingly in favor of sharing, but this would be voluntary, and no one would be forced to participate.

Early in the morning just five days before the first official repatriation under the agreement, people from around the refuge converged on the sub-camp Copinol to participate in preparing for the departure of half the people there. The houses had to be taken apart, and the lumber, doors, and gal-vanized roof panels stacked in a way that would facilitate loading onto the trucks. Hundreds of people were working, with crowbars and hammers, bringing down roofs, walls, upright supports. Dozens more were carrying lumber to a storage area, where others supervised stacking. Some people (mostly children) wandered through the work area, picking up nails and put-ting them into barrels and sacks to be reused in Meanguera.

As the dwellings came down around them, the beds were left in place; the families would sleep *a pura pampa* (in the open air) for the next few nights. There was no threat of rain, though the norte might return at any time, and the nights were cold. But the excitement about the impending return made the arrangement seem more an adventure than a sacrifice. "When we came here, we slept under the trees and the stars because we had nothing. Now we're doing it again, but this time it's because we're going home. We're very happy. We're going back to our country, to our land." Most of the people stayed for the remaining days in the space their viviendas had occupied—the outlines of the rooms were visible in the dirt.

Personal possessions such as tables, shelves, water containers, boxes and bags for packing, and beds had long been marked with the owner's name, subcamp, and colonia. Now everything but beds and a few personal items were packed into large net bags or boxes, or tied up in bundles, in preparation for loading. This activity started while the houses were still being taken apart.

In the midst of this noisy, dirty, sweaty, and generally festive environment of well-organized chaos, some of the women cooked tortillas and meals and baked various breads in the collective ovens to take along on the journey. The family hens and roosters, creatures of habit, ran in a panic for the slopes, where later they were found and tied up with the family's other possessions. Children played in the midst of all the activity, or helped pack or collect nails. Family members from other subcamps came to visit and send off the people in Copinol.

By the middle of the following day, most of the packing was done. Now a little apprehension set in. UNHCR was contracting with Honduran truck owners and drivers at that very late moment to provide a hundred vehicles. Would the trucks really come? All of them? On time? Would the plans be adequate to control this extraordinary amount of traffic? Would the governments or UNHCR present any last-minute obstacles?

Three days later, the trucks started to come into the refuge. Before entering, each had been given a number and an identification sticker by UNHCR; at the cabin at the entrance to the camp they were registered by the refugees, who gave each one another number, a sign indicating which of the four settlements in Meanguera would be its destination, and instructions for parking and loading. That day, the majority of the trucks were loaded with lumber and other building supplies; machinery, equipment, and materials from the workshops, schools, clinics, gardens, and animal barns; food and seeds for Meanguera; and household and personal goods. That same afternoon, some journalists and diplomats started arriving in the village of Colomoncagua.

Before dawn on January 14, the refugees of colonias I through V of Copinol arranged themselves and their baggage to be loaded onto twenty open trucks. The sides of the trucks were hung with large banners reflecting the mood of the community: Salvadoran Brothers: Nine Years of Exile, Nine Years of Experience; Living in Community Is the Guarantee of Our Development; Honduran People: We Thank You for Your Hospitality, Nine Years of Exile Demonstrate It; We Will Work As a Community to Develop a New Productive Life in Meanguera. After loading, the trucks proceeded through the refuge to the tranca, where each one unloaded its passengers; the refugees passed through a Honduran immigration check, a Salvadoran immigra-

Primary school class under the trees, Los Hatos I, March 1990.

tion check, and a UNHCR check, where they received their cash benefits. Then they remounted the truck, which meanwhile had been passed through the tranca by the Honduran military.

When all the trucks had gone through this process, they left in a jubilant procession followed by a handful of cars filled with agency personnel, visitors, journalists, and religious workers. The foreigners were all given permission to enter El Salvador with the refugees and stay in Meanguera with them for two days. The procession passed through the village of Colomon-cagua, where they were greeted by numerous waving residents, and then on to the border crossing at Las Flores.

After nine long years of exile, the refugees were returning to El Salvador. Out of their stay in the desert, where they had transformed themselves into a new kind of community, they were crossing over to their Canaan.

▲   ▲   ▲

The caravan arrived a few hours later in Meanguera, where those who had gone before were waiting to greet them with *frescos* (fruit drinks), banners, and embraces. For the first few nights, they would sleep under communal tent canopies, or under the stars, while they searched for their belongings and constructed the *champas* (huts) of tree limbs, thatch, and nylon sheeting that would be their first, temporary, shelters.

The physical conditions were in some important respects inferior to what they had left in Colomoncagua: they would live in huts; there were virtually no buildings; everything remained to be built. Of course, some of the con-ditions were better—there was more land, the soil in Meanguera is very fertile, and the cold and crystalline little La Joya River runs through the settlements, providing a place to bathe that the newly repatriated people rushed to enjoy. Despite the difficulties immediately ahead, the very notable mood was one of relief, determination, and joy.

And, of course, there are other conditions besides physical ones. Within hours of arriving, some of the youngsters had been dispatched to the neigh-boring villages to buy bananas or oranges, or to the hills to pick mangoes. Those first pieces of fruit carried an almost inconceivable burden of sym-bolic meanings. First, they represented the right to move freely wherever one wished: to town, to another village, to visit family, for a walk in the hills or along the road, to hitch a ride to San Miguel or San Salvador. Soon enough the refugees would have to confront the realities of military restric-tions when they crossed the river; for the moment they saw that they could come and go, they could leave the settlement, they could breathe freely.

Second, the fruit represented the freedom to make choices: Now we can buy the kinds of bananas or oranges that strike our fancy, not just accept whatever is provided by UNHCR or an agency donation. Or we can decide where we want to go to pick the fruit—what joy! (One newly repatriated man described going with a group of friends to look at some nearby land and finding a group of kids under a mango tree. Bellies swollen and happy, they had stripped most of the fruit from the tree.)

Finally, fruit itself had been in short supply in Colomoncagua, and had been sorely missed during the long years of exile. Getting hold of some now represented the availability of things, simple things to be sure, which are part of the richness that the life of poor peasants can also provide.

When a truck stops on the road, people run up to ask the driver for a ride—a common means of transportation throughout rural Central America. This truck is in San Luís, on the calle negra, the road that runs through the new settlement.

So the fruit represented the regaining of freedom, the return to home, the hopes for the future. Little wonder that for the next few weeks, until the season ended, the community went a little crazy in what one ex-refugee later called "the euphoria of the oranges."

Over the ensuing weeks, the same process of repatriation would be repeated thirteen times. By early March, the camp at Colomoncagua was deserted and the entire community resettled in Meanguera. They were living in champas, waiting for the new town to be laid out, plots to be assigned, and construction of provisional houses to begin. The workshops were not yet functioning. It was clear that planting community crops would have to be put off for a year, and a project was developed through PADECOMSM with neighboring communities to provide corn and beans for the first year. The health system had begun to organize itself, and sanitation and preventive care were under way, but there was not yet a building for the lab. There were no chapels yet. The collective kitchens were functioning, even though some did not have roofs and were set up under the trees. School started for the children in February, also under the trees. The guarderías were active. The water system was being worked on, although piping water to all the settlements was still in the future. The electric generators were not yet set up. The mechanical workshop was operating only in a limited way.

The newly repatriated community was not thinking about regaining what they had in Colomoncagua, but instead launching something that had never been seen in Morazán. The moment was one of preparation: preparing the fields, the layout of the town, the physical infrastructure, the new social, political, and economic structures. People in the community talked to visitors with great optimism. The atmosphere was one of expectation. The community was like a great cat, coiled, muscles strong and flexed, ready to spring forward.

In the new settlement, the community would have to become more self-reliant. This suited their plans—the move from the harsh but assisted environment of Colomoncagua to integration into what they saw as "reality" was their goal—but in any event, it was necessary. The agencies that had given them so much help in the camp were not all available to them in Morazán—they did not have permission from the Salvadoran government to work there, or they did not have missions in that country, or for any number of reasons. The refugees were, in a sense, being thrown into the pool, and would have to start swimming on their own very quickly.

MSF was there with a small emergency mission; the staff seemed eager to cooperate with the community, and the conflicts in Honduras were forgotten. Lutheran World Federation, the international humanitarian agency of the Lutheran countries, had one representative in the settlement. And UNHCR was there, helping the repatriated community as much as possible. The UNHCR staff, too, seemed very dedicated to the community and the tasks before them. So there was a strong sense of support, but the personnel and the resources were far fewer than the community had been able to rely on in Honduras.

The Salvadoran government and military criticized the ex-refugees for their decision to return to a zone of "high conflict." Generally, the area of Morazán north of the Torola River was—and is—understood to be under the control of the rebel FMLN. This does not mean that the government army cannot enter the zone, but to do so they must disembark from helicopters or send large numbers of men, and even then can only stay temporarily, until the FMLN decides to engage them.

In December 1989, visitors from the United States asked some refugees if they were not nervous about going into an FMLN-controlled zone. One answered, "No. Remember, it was the government army that drove us from our homes in the first place. The FMLN has never killed our family members, burned our houses, or driven us out, only the army. If we return to the government-controlled areas that [Vice-President] Merino proposed, do you know what will happen? In a couple of months, all our projects will be destroyed by sabotage and harassment. We don't want to throw out nine years of work like that."

Clearly, many in the community sympathize with the rebels for fighting against the very system that oppressed them and drove them into exile. This does not mean that the new settlement was an FMLN center. There were no FMLN soldiers to be seen there. Nor were there any guns. The community knew that the government had spies among them. A leader told us, "One of our commercial people was in Corado's office [the commander of the Fourth Military Detachment] to talk about some permissions, and Corado showed him a file with every single newsletter and bulletin we have put out since we came back. They know everything we do." The presence of combatants or weapons would not long go undetected in such an open environment.

The community was very clear that the success of their project depended on maintaining independence from the fighting and from reliance on either of what they call "the two bands." The FMLN respected their position, and the attempts by the military to take advantage of their presence to reassert government control over the area were minor. The government army was less circumspect than the FMLN about entering the new settlement, however. On January 15, the day after the first official repatriation, a small group headed by a sergeant entered the settlement of Los Hatos and started to ask for some people by name. But there were no major incidents in the first months after the return of the population.

▲   ▲   ▲

Just before leaving the camp at Colomoncagua, the community had issued a statement of gratitude to the many individuals and organizations that helped them during their long years of exile. To UNHCR and the other agencies, the community wrote:

> Nine years in a refugee camp is a long time. The truth is that we don't know what would have happened to us if we had been here alone. But we haven't been alone. From the beginning UNHCR and the international humanitarian agencies have accompanied us. It hasn't just been the agencies as institutions, but the people the agencies have sent here. People who have shared our hardships and joys, who have worked hard and who have taught us. Each of these people has given us all that they could. . . .

To all the people who have been unknown to us but who have supported us from within their own countries, making our cause their own:

To all the people who have visited us and who have gone back to their communities to let people know about our situation and our life here:

It is very difficult for us after nine years to express in words our feelings. Perhaps the best way is simply to say: MANY THANKS FOR EVERYTHING. Thanks because we have been able to see the reality of the words: SOLIDARITY AMONG THE PEOPLES OF THE WORLD.

A NEW CITY IS LAUNCHED

"Now we are no longer refugees. We do not want to return to being refugees, and that demands that we look for the path to our reintegration into normal life. We want to reproduce the experience of the refuge, but not to reproduce another refugee camp in El Salvador."

Even as the physical and institutional infrastructure of the new town was being developed, the community had to begin to confront important political and economic concerns. The most important first task was to avoid isolation. The government had promised free transit and commerce between Meanguera and the rest of the country, and the community immediately began to test that commitment. Delegations were sent to cities in the eastern zone, as well as to San Salvador, to meet with government and international agencies, to make purchases and invite businesspeople to Meanguera, and to confer with the press.

The main problem they encountered was that in that region the army, not the government, really ruled. The repatriated refugees would have to negotiate and struggle for the same concessions from the military that they had already supposedly won from the government. In Morazán, everyone leaving the main city, San Francisco Gotera, was stopped at a military checkpoint. If they were carrying goods they had purchased, they would have to show their permission to bring those goods farther north. If they were not from the region, they would have to show their permission to travel.

"They even control goods on the supposedly 'free' list—basic foods, and so on," explained a member of a provisional leadership group in the settlement. "What we say is, having to ask permission to bring food here is like having to ask permission to eat."

The approach the community adopted was determined, but calm, firmness:

One man had gone to Gotera and bought shoes for his kids. The sergeant at the *retén* (checkpoint) told him he could not carry that much clothing—only what the kids were wearing. He became very sad and asked the sergeant to do him the favor of letting him take the stuff. That pitiful attitude seemed to enrage the soldiers, and the situation became worse. So we don't use pity, or anger—just firmness.

Sometimes they stop one of our vehicles that has gone in to shop. The people know they have the right to pass, so they don't argue at all; they just get down and sit by the side of the road, sometimes for hours. Finally, the soldiers let them through. Meanwhile, our people take advantage of the situation and start to talk to the soldiers—not political speeches, just conversations about what we're doing here, about life. And the soldiers also say what they are thinking. So we are opening dialogues.

One of the issues the community raised with the government was the construction of a new bridge over the Torola River, which serves as the effective

The bridge over the Torola River, which linked northern Morazán to the rest of the country until it was blown up in 1983. Replacing it was a high priority for the returning community.

border between government- and FMLN-controlled zones in Morazán. The bridge had been blown up by the rebels in 1983. Replacing it was crucial to the community's future integration into the national economy; although the river could be waded or forded by vehicles in the dry season (when the community arrived), once the rains came this would be impossible. The army offered to build a replacement bridge, but demanded that the community create a civil defense patrol to guard it. The people felt that this would make the bridge an FMLN target again, and in any event would increase military control over their lives. They proposed that money be raised by international agencies to build the bridge. The topic was discussed without formal resolution during the first period after repatriation.

Meanwhile, the community was moving toward what they called the "reactivation" of the economic institutions developed in Colomoncagua. New agencies and enterprises were established. One was the Committee for Development and Emergency in Morazán (CODEMO), charged with establishing the economic base necessary to maintain the community in four general areas of production: agriculture, livestock, industry, and crafts. The plan was to begin with much the same structure as in the camp. The workshops and other productive areas would be maintained as communal activities, with the profits from the sale of products used to support "nonproductive" services such as education and health and to provide for the elderly and for children—who were no longer working in the shops, but attending school full time.

As the work areas became more productive, stable, and self-supporting, and the political structure of the new settlement established its legitimacy as a municipal government, there would be three important changes. The economic enterprises would convert to autonomous cooperatives, run by the worker/members. Workers would receive salaries from the profits of the enterprise, rather than the initial token disbursements. Later, when they developed a new, legally recognized, municipal government, it would be able to support social services by levying taxes. But this was all for the future.

Another agency was launched to develop commercial relationships between Meanguera (and indeed all of northern Morazán) and the rest of the country, called the Committee for Commercial Development (CODECO). It was responsible for developing a market, both local and national, for the products of the various work areas and for creating a structure to provide the supplies the community needed, both for production and for daily necessities in the short run.

Because the resources at the community's disposal, although objectively quite limited, were greater than they had ever been, the plan incorporated buying things at wholesale to sell at reduced prices in new stores, providing supplies to producers, and even negotiating with government agencies for the provision of services and benefits in the area.

Finally, the Communal Bank of Morazán (BANCOMO), what we would call a thrift institution or credit union, had already been started before the people left Colomoncagua. Capitalized with savings accounts (people were asked to deposit half of what UNHCR had given them, and some had money they had received from relatives abroad) and with donations, the bank was to invest in community projects, channel financial contributions from outside the area, and help the new enterprises and other structures handle their books and accounts.

One small enterprise was launched even while the repatriations were happening: a *comedor* (diner), similar to countless rural Central American places to eat, at the side of the road near the northern limit of the settlement. It was run by a middle-aged woman who had worked in a nutrition center in Colomoncagua. She described the way the comedor operated:

> We're doing o.k. During the last repatriation, the truck drivers and the internationals all ate here. And the drivers going to Gualcho. Also, MSF eats here, and the ones who are hauling water in the government tank trucks. People from the other communities on the way to Perquín or Jocoaitique stop to eat here. Sometimes, someone from within the community, too.
>
> We get tortillas from the collective kitchen. They're functioning here, just like in the camp—they make tortillas and beans, and the rest everyone makes as they wish.
>
> Our prices are by conscience, depending on the meal. A meal costs five colones or three and a half. But if someone comes in from the community, and we know they don't have money, we charge them less. And [grinning] if it's a truck driver or an international, we charge more. Or sometimes an old person, or a pregnant woman, or a kid, comes in, and I just give them something to eat. So it's based on conscience.
>
> So we're making some money. We give it to the leadership. It's used to buy what we need here. There's a shopping committee; they go to San Miguel or San Salvador to get what we need.
>
> We don't get a salary yet. It's like in the camps—we work here, and we get everything we need. Later, we'll get a salary from the profits.

▲   ▲   ▲

A group of leaders of the community are discussing some of the early incidents indicating the need to assimilate into society. The newly repatriated people found that they had changed during their years in exile, in some ways that were visible from the outside, and in other ways that were more evident internally.

They looked like hicks—they all dressed the same, in the clothes that were made in the camp. In the zone, a visitor could often spot a repatriated person by these garments, especially the striped socks and heavy work shoes, which were made in the workshops and have a distinctive Colomoncagua look.

"When we go into town, we walk together. We are inexperienced in buying things, in moving in the towns. Sometimes people don't know to ask for lower prices, so they end up paying more than they have to."

Tomás E. explains, "We have to learn new habits, because we are tied to the habits we learned in the camp, but we are confronting reality. Here's an example: maybe a group will be walking together in town, and one guy wants to buy a candy. He doesn't have enough to buy for everyone, just for himself. But we are used to sharing everything equally. So, rather than have something the rest don't have, he doesn't buy the thing."

Mabel R., who had come in the November repatriation, laughs and puts in her contribution: "Money is a real change. Over there [in Colomoncagua] we weren't used to going around with money. Everything was given out, or you asked for something. If there was a car going to another subcamp, you just got on." Here she giggles, a little embarrassed. "Often we didn't even say 'thank you,' or else we thanked the driver and that was it. However, here, everything has to be paid for. People go to Gotera and say, 'And over there, do they give out water?' But no, everything is for sale. Bit by bit, we're getting used to paying, because nothing is given away."

Another person in the group adds, "We can't go into a comedor together, because it feels odd for each one to order their own food." And, to general laughter, "It almost seems it would be easier if everyone ate by themselves. But this is rigid behavior. We want to preserve the values that are expressed, but lose the rigidity."

"The other day," says José, "a truck went to Gotera to make some purchases. The people don't know about driving in the city [actually, an indication of how much they had advanced in Colomoncagua. Some people learned how to drive there, but as they had never had the opportunity before, they didn't know all the rules of the road]. They went the wrong way down a one-way street. The police arrived, and there was a big argument. They wanted to arrest them, and they even said they were drunk. Then they gave them a ticket. To them, this ticket was just a piece of paper, and I told them, 'Keep that paper.' I'm telling them, 'You have to pay the fine, because if you don't, you'll have to pay it when we go to register the vehicle again.'"

Catalina asks, "And where do you go to pay it?"

"The same place where you get the registration papers."

"And where is that, in San Salvador?"

José, a high-level leader of the community, smiles and shrugs, "Who *knows* where it is!"

In the community's comedor, on the side of the road, doña María explains to a visitor that there have been other changes as well.

> After our experience, one feels somehow different. It's not like before, when one's friendships were only with the family, with

one's cousins, with one's aunts and uncles, or brothers and sisters. Now the friendship is communal. This is something I feel.

We visited family in San Fernando. They received us well; they had a ceremony, they gave us food. We slept in their houses—one night here, another night there. There was confidence. But I didn't really feel tranquil; in the night, I felt afraid. I didn't want to sit or lie down. I didn't feel fully comfortable until I came back here.

There is a special confidence here. I think that's why the people are staying so close together.

"Even if it's true that this is a community of 100 percent campesino origins, the values we have created don't allow us to live in the same way," explains José, one of the community leaders. "For example, here everyone had the choice of where to settle, where to put their champa, and what is surprising is that the first thing that happened was that everyone grouped together. There was a lot of land where we could have spread out, but no, the tendency has been to stay together."

Some of the newly repatriated families began to build houses, even before the land was laid out. Asked if people would be allowed to settle outside the lots assigned to them, Tomás answers, "Look, some people have already moved back to where they used to live, and some have gone to where they found a nice spot for a house. Once the lots are drawn, they will still have the right to do that, but it will be more difficult for them to get services—water, electricity, materials for the houses in the plan. But even that may be possible; anyway, they are free to choose. If you look around on Sundays, you'll see groups of people visiting where they used to live, looking at their old houses, the burned houses, where they had families."

José adds, "The thing is, the main reason we returned in colonias and subcamps was to facilitate the organization of the move; here people are free to change their colonia, to live near friends or relatives. Sometimes they don't seem to realize that. But whoever wants to can move. We don't want to re-create the conditions of a closed camp—this is not a closed or rigid place."

▲   ▲   ▲

Before they left Colomoncagua, the refugees knew that important conditions would change for them in Meanguera. "We knew we would move from being an assisted community to a community in development." They were conscious of criticism that the governance structure they had developed, for all its strengths, did not provide sufficiently direct representation. "We wanted to move from a stepwise representation to a more direct election of authority." As a preparatory step, the Asamblea de Comités approved a new political structure, called "popular democracy," for the new settlement, which was to be named Ciudad Segundo Montes. Even as they were erecting

their dwellings, meetings would be organized by colonia to elect representatives to a new Asamblea General (general assembly), one representative
for every two colonias, or about forty in all. The Asamblea General, which
would be the highest political authority in the new structure, was to elect a
Junta Directiva (leadership board), which would in turn select the members
of a new Unidad Ejecutora (executive unit), responsible for day-to-day administration and for coordinating the work of five administrative bodies:
CODEMO, CODECO, BANCOMO, and two others.

These two were the Urban Development Commission, responsible for
overseeing the development of plans, the construction of dwellings and other
buildings, the creation of the water and electrical systems—in general,
everything that had to do with the physical urban infrastructure of the new
city; and the Communal Commission, in charge of community services
(health, education, sanitation, and other areas of public assistance), community organizations, activities in the sectors, and pastoral work.

The new structure might be translated into United States political terms as
a kind of hybrid between the city council/city manager system of municipal
government (although with much smaller constituencies for each council
member) and the town meeting.

The newly repatriated community had a clear sense of the larger significance of what they were trying to do. They believed that their ability to re-
develop the model they had in the camp, and to integrate successfully into
the national economy and society, would have important consequences for
northern Morazán, and beyond that for the eastern region of the country, and
indeed for El Salvador as a whole.

First, the economic development of the settlement was tied to that of the
entire zone. They had brought with them trades that were unknown in the
zone; for the first time, such things as shoes, tools, and clothing would be
produced in a cost-effective way for a local market, which in a reasonable
time would include all of northern Morazán. Similarly, their trade in these
goods with the economic centers of San Salvador and San Miguel would
result in an economic integration affecting the entire area. The community
owned several donated and purchased vehicles and ran a mechanical workshop, which would also contribute to the availability of goods throughout
the zone.

Also, in the community, both the stores (which they had experimented
with in a very small way in Colomoncagua) and the production workshops
were seen primarily as community services. Taking advantage of econo-
mies of scale and needing only to cover administrative costs (and someday,
wages), they could develop the income they required while maintaining low
prices. This, they believed, would have repercussions for the availability of
goods at prices the overall community could afford.

Agricultural programs would in the long run increase the availability of
some foods. In the case of eggs, this began to happen almost immediately.
One leader explained, "In Perquín, eggs cost sixty centavos; here the granja

charges thirty-five. Already people have started to come from some of the towns to buy eggs. Of course, we can't satisfy the demand yet, but we will do better. And in the short run, we will have an effect on the prices in the whole area—they'll have to try to lower their costs to meet our prices."

Also, a project of corn and bean silage was established to provide supplies throughout the year. This will stabilize prices, which have had a yearly cycle, so that at some times people in the area could not afford the most basic food items. "Actually," one of the people working in economic re-activation pointed out, "the new stores, the local production of goods, the availability of transport, and the silage program are important because as poor as the people are here, the main obstacle to their getting goods is not their cost, but the lack of access."

Second, the social programs of the community would have direct implications for the zone. Teachers were already being sent to various nearby communities to help in primary education, where they were greeted enthusiastically. Two sisters who started to teach in a small, isolated village, explained:

> When we arrived, there was a meeting. PADECOMS proposed that some of us should go to help raise the cultural level of our brothers in some of the villages. We felt content to go and help other people. And we felt good again when we got there and saw the joy of the people—they were happy to have us there. There was a community meeting to welcome us. Because of the lack of teachers, they had not been able to develop education as it should be. There was just one class for the early grades. I work in the third grade; she is in the second. The parents thank us for having come; they seem very grateful. We live there with a family and only come home every other weekend. The people treat us very well—they come to visit us, bring us food, more than we need. I'm happy to be there.

The development of health programs and other services would similarly benefit the entire zone. It could not be otherwise; the emergence of Ciudad Segundo Montes as a privileged community surrounded by poorer villages and towns might seem perfectly normal from a United States perspective, but in Morazán it would be a totally untenable situation. And in any event, it was not in their plans. They saw themselves as a focus for the development—social, economic, and political—of all of Morazán, not just their own town.

The repatriation of the community from Colomoncagua was followed by the repopulation of the nearby town of Arambala. Virtually abandoned after government bombings in the early eighties, it saw a return by the former residents. Thus, there was hope that the repatriation might be tied to a general repopulation of the zone.

The political struggle against isolation was tied to the general security of the civilian population in the zone. The presence and activism of the repatriated community had some immediate security benefits. People felt more secure in general; they returned to using the *calle negra,* the paved road, which had been abandoned because of fear. The struggle to be able to bring goods, both personal and communal, into the zone, past the retén at Gotera, had implications for the entire area.

There were incidents immediately that suggested people were feeling more secure because of the presence of the repatriated refugees. "Once, a few days ago," a member of the community recounted, "soldiers stopped a bus near Gotera and made everyone get off. Then they separated the repatriated people from the rest and told the rest they could go. They started to say, 'But why do the others have to stay? We all live in the same area.' Then everyone started to argue with the soldiers, and they gave in and let everyone go." Every victory they achieved in the area of free transit or free commerce implied a limitation on the arbitrary powers of the military and new openings throughout the nation.

The repatriated community communicated regularly through press conferences, paid advertising, and their own publications. They encouraged visits and worked closely with other communities and grass-roots organizations in El Salvador. In this way, they hoped that people would become aware of what they were doing, so that the settlement might serve as a model for rural economic and social development for the entire country.

THE DEDICATION OF THE NEW CITY

> "Our community wants to contribute to peace, building schools, attending to health, creating sources of work, producing so that we might live better; for nine years we lived with assistance and we prepared ourselves for this moment."

On March 25, 1990, the day after the tenth anniversary of the murder of Msgr. Oscar A. Romero, the new community of Ciudad Segundo Montes was dedicated in a public ceremony in the *asentimiento* (settlement) of El Quebrachal. The day began with the arrival at about ten o'clock of a procession from the nearby town of Jocoaitique. Between five hundred and a thousand residents of the surrounding communities of northern Morazán participated in this spirited march, carrying banners commemorating the anniversary of the martyrdom of Msgr. Romero and others and welcoming the recently repatriated community.

During the preceding days, numbers of Salvadoran visitors, mostly relatives of the repatriates and merchants setting up stands for the celebration, had been arriving. The atmosphere was festive. A generator and a temporary lighting system had been set up. Two water trucks bringing drinking water from a spring at some distance were provided by the government.

Billboard honoring Dr. Segundo Montes and a permanent plaque in his honor. At the ceremony dedicating Ciudad Segundo Montes, El Quebrachal subcamp, March 25, 1990.

After the procession, delegations of foreign visitors, international agencies, and Salvadoran popular organizations started arriving from San Salvador in cars, trucks, and buses. In the midst of all the activity, a caravan of vehicles filled with supplies—tools, food, powdered milk, medicines—organized by the U.S.-based Pastors for Peace arrived. The caravan was the product of months of work in the United States, with numerous organizations across the country collecting money to purchase the seven trucks and supplies to fill them. The announcement of its arrival provoked an enthusiastic and grateful welcome from the crowd.

And, of course, a large number of people from the community attended. It was a hot day, and there was a constant flow of people seeking shade and water away from the field where the activities were held, but there were always a few thousand people in the field from about eleven o'clock on.

By late morning, the ceremonies had begun. From the newly constructed stage, there were addresses by Juan José Rodríguez, one of the leaders of the community; Carlos Castro, of PADECOES, an organization of economic and social cooperatives throughout the country; José María Tojeira, a representative of the Jesuits in El Salvador; and Romeo Piñeda Reyes, the

Carlos Castro of PADECOES speaking at the dedication.

Children from the community curiously confronting one of the troops sent to "protect" the army officers during the dedication ceremony.

Newly repatriated women listening to speeches at the dedication.

ARENA governor of Morazán Department. On the one hand, the community and their allies were declaring their existence and insisting that the government live up to the agreements to allow free transit and free commerce between their zone and the rest of the country. On the other hand, the government was offering thinly veiled threats about the consequences of straying from "law and order" and the "unfortunate" decision to relocate in a war zone, where "the government couldn't protect them." Still, as the community had planned and hoped, the atmosphere was relaxed and cordial.

After the speeches, there was an ecumenical prayer service, led by various local clergy as well as by Father Miguel Francisco Estrada, the new rector of the Universidad Centroamericana; the Reverend Medardo Gómez, the bishop of the Lutheran church in El Salvador; Father Pedro Casaldáliga of Brazil, the well-known promoter of liberation theology; and others.

During the prayer service, combat-dressed and -equipped soldiers of the Fourth Military Detachment, headquartered in nearby Gotera, began to

People running from the dust storm created by the helicopter's downwash.

appear in the crowd, painting their faces with camouflage and roaming throughout the area. Before long it was clear that they were there in serious numbers—over one hundred. The reason for their presence, which both fascinated and disconcerted the community but did not interrupt the proceedings, became clear after a while. In a roaring cloud of dust, a helicopter arrived and landed at the edge of the field, disgorging the commander of the Fourth Military Detachment, Colonel Corado; his second, Colonel Tejada; and a United States sergeant who spent the rest of his time trying to pretend he was a Salvadoran, despite his terrible Spanish. Colonel Corado had been invited by the community and addressed a few words to the crowd, seconding the menacing message of the governor. But their threatening could not destroy the positive and enthusiastic tone of the day.

Short addresses by members of some delegations, songs by the conjunto, and the unveiling of a plaque dedicating the new city to the memory of the

murdered Jesuit priest, Dr. Segundo Montes, concluded the formal ceremonies, and the thousands in attendance retired to welcome frescos, water,
and sandwiches.

Later, there were cultural performances, and a tree was planted to com-
memorate the event. Finally, about eight in the evening the conjunto started
playing dance music, and the community and their visitors gathered on the
big field where the ceremony had been held. The dancing raised a tremen-
dous dust cloud, and at about ten o'clock there was an announcement from
the stage that one of the government water trucks was coming to wet down
the ground. The crowd parted for the truck, and the driver took out a big
hose and started spraying, to the delight of the people, who amid shouting
and general hilarity, ran and ducked out of the way of the stream. It had been
a long, hot day, and people were tired. The band had been playing between
speeches since about ten that morning—the strain could be heard in their
voices. But this was a very special day. People continued to dance until three
in the morning.

The people had returned to their promised land, where their new city had
been launched.

CHAPTER

5

CREATING A NEW LIFE IN MORAZÁN

▲▲▲

What people want here is a total change from a way of living before, communal living. Before, we didn't have the ability to decide even to have a clinic. We didn't have the education, the learning, the technical training. We lived in hunger and misery. We didn't know what to do to change that way of life. Now we have found the path to follow so that all of us will have a better way of life.

By the end of June 1990, a new one-lane bridge over the Torola River linked Ciudad Segundo Montes with the rest of El Salvador. Built by the Salvadoran government after months of pressure, the gleaming silver structure meant that pedestrian and vehicular traffic into northern Morazán was once again possible. By early July, a regular commercial bus line had extended its route across the river, and trucks were able to bring in supplies for the community and nearby towns in northern Morazán. Both symbolically and literally, a critical link with the rest of the country had been forged.

For many in the community, being back in El Salvador meant seeing people they'd lost contact with a decade before, discovering loved ones long feared dead. "When we opened the warehouse in Gotera, I was coordinating putting the shipment of food into the building," a man in his fifties told us. "It was about 5:30 in the afternoon. . . . All of a sudden I saw a couple of people, who ran up to me and embraced me. They were my cousins and my father's godchildren. They were from Mozote. I didn't think those people existed any more; I thought they were dead."

After nine years of exile and incarceration in Honduras, the community rejoiced in being able to come and go as they pleased, in seeing familiar places, in reunions with loved ones, in working the *milpa*, the cornfield that

Overleaf: Champas in Quebrachos. The residents are waiting for their provisional houses to be built.

is such a central part of campesino culture. Early in the morning, streams of people walked up the calle negra on their way to tend the milpa, carrying *cumas*, the large, curved knives used in agriculture. They would work in the family plots before and after going to their jobs, and at the end of the day might bring back some cucumbers, *pipián* (a squash), or a basket of *frijoles* or green beans. In the evening, they would sharpen the cumas for the next day's work.

"Nothing takes away from our joy of being here in El Salvador," we were told over and over. Although it had been expected that many would leave the community to go back to land they owned or move in with family in nearby villages, this did not happen. One group of a hundred left to form agricultural cooperatives in adjacent areas, but this extended the community's influence rather than weakening it. "It's an advance, like a beehive sending out a new colony. This is part of our plan," Alejandro, one of the community's leaders, explained.

Their cohesiveness remained intact, despite the loosening of the external constraints that had made unity so critical in Colomoncagua. "We have a lot of land near Guacamaya," commented don Visitación. "Nobody uses it now. But we wouldn't want to be alone, apart from the community. There's nobody in that whole zone to the east of here. It's frightening to walk through there—no roosters crowing, no dogs barking, just a lot of deer." Another family described their plans to move to land they own farther up the road so they can watch over their pineapples. Asked how they felt about leaving the community, they said, "We won't!" The grandmother explained, "The girls will come here every day to work. We'll only live there, but come here all the time."

Margarita, a woman working in food distribution, indicated how deeply the community's ideas had been changed by their experiences in the camp. "Before, we didn't live like this; we lived in houses very far apart. Some lived where no one came to visit, they were so far away. But in Colomoncagua, we always were so many people together. It's been our dream, since we left there to come here, to stay together, not to separate again."

The move from Colomoncagua to Meanguera represented more than a physical relocation. These people had gone from the dependent, assisted condition of refugees, through the status of a repatriating community—motivated by their own vision but still receiving assistance for the actual move—to the situation they had wanted and worked for, as an independent, self-governing community preparing to assume its role in the economic, social, and political life of the nation.

The refugee camp, while in many ways a prison, had also sheltered them from certain harsh features of normal life. As refugees, they were guaranteed a minimal level of resources—food, housing, firewood, materials for their workshops—by the agencies that had formal responsibility for their welfare. At the same time, they were unable to make fundamental decisions about their lives, and thus were deprived of the opportunity to test their plans and capabilities in experience. Their accomplishments in the refuge had been

In the new granja for laying hens, constructed and put into operation immediately upon arriving in Meanguera.

won under conditions of great hardship but also under a kind of artificial protection, which provided an almost utopian laboratory environment.

Now that they had won freedom and independence, they had achieved both the right and the necessity to support themselves, to make their own decisions. They were moving rapidly from dependency to development, identifying new expectations, understanding new needs, and learning new skills as they went. But it was not an easy process for them. "A ter nine years of being in a refuge, receiving assistance, a mentality is created of the assisted person. After nine years, you don't change that pattern overnight. It's a great struggle," admitted Darío, coordinator of the community's development structure, CODEMO.

The repatriated refugees were acutely aware of the significance of their new situation of independence. They also understood that without outside assistance their project would not succeed. Aid was now conditional on their skills as proposal writers, negotiators, and advocates for their own cause. They were grateful for the assistance of several internationals who had worked as agency staff in Colomoncagua and became trusted allies, co-workers, and consultants. And they worked closely with Salvadoran developmental organizations such as FASTRAS and PADECOMSM, which provided technical and material assistance for specific projects. Within weeks of repatriation, an office had been set up in San Salvador; here they had computers, telephones, a photocopier, even a fax machine to communicate with funding sources, development organizations, and government agencies.

Running the office illustrated the enormity of the challenge the community was taking on. To prepare staff to work in the capital, people who had lived all their lives in remote rural areas had to be taught such urban skills as ordering and paying for meals in restaurants, using buses and taxis, negotiating the hectic streets of San Salvador, operating kitchen and bathroom appliances, using the telephone and fax, and so forth. "One of the most difficult things is that we never go outside," one leader told us. "We have to spend the whole day cooped up indoors!"

The confrontation with reality that characterized the experience of the community after repatriation was both exhilarating and difficult. Some important projects required much more time than had been foreseen. For example, the original plan was to move everyone into provisional *viviendas mínimas* (minimal dwellings) before the rains began in earnest in May. But the process of laying out lots extended over months, delaying the construction of the little wooden houses, so that some families had to spend the entire rainy season in the plastic-covered champas. Goals had to be reassessed as limitations were encountered and addressed.

Priority was given to meeting basic needs and to minimizing the unevenness of the infrastructure of the five asentimientos that make up the city: El Quebrachal (sometimes also called Quebrachos), San Luis, Los Hatos I and II, and El Barrial. The latter, in a particularly lovely location, only recently had water piped in and was still isolated by the terrible road, passable only by the sturdiest of the community's several vehicles. Some people had moved out of El Barrial to other asentimientos because of these problems,

In the new granja for laying hens, constructed and put into operation immediately upon arriving in Meanguera.

but most put up with the difficulties with customary good humor. Generally, morale remained high in the community, despite the slowness of progress and setbacks in some areas.

In some ways, the transition to reality conflicted with the utopian values that guided the community. For example, certain economic differences among people began to emerge, reflecting the introduction of commerce and the undeniable fact of unequal means. Some families had relatives who sent them money, so they could afford a radio, nicer clothes, supplemental food, or occasional snacks bought from street vendors or the little stores set up in the community. Others had only the few things they had brought with them from Colomoncagua, and their only source of funds was the token salary of twenty-five colones a month. A few bananas or a bus ride to Perquín cost one colón; even an occasional *charamusca,* the popular fruit ice sold in tiny plastic bags, was a treat beyond the reach of many families. Those with greater resources—and resourcefulness—had already invested in a pig, hoping to fatten it for sale or to sell piglets, or were lucky enough to purchase a goat or even a cow. "You have to think about your resources," said Vicente A., a thoughtful and soft-spoken man who served as a guide for visitors. "We always said that buying a pig was like having a bank account."

Differences in personal possessions were not great, however, so the general environment of the community was still one of basic equality. As one leader pointed out, even at this early stage, "There is no other place in this country where a family has guaranteed the things they're guaranteed here." Health care and education were provided to all, without charge. The most critical resources—housing, land, workplaces—were collectively owned and equitably distributed. The new viviendas under construction were simple one-room wooden shacks with dirt floors and corrugated tin roofs, varying only by the size of the household. These structures and the lots will remain the property of the community, to be used by the occupants so long as they or their families live there. And the factories, yet to be built, will continue to be owned by the community as a whole, although they might become autonomous cooperatives once they achieve economic self-sufficiency.

All members of the community were still entitled to basic food donated by foreign governments and agencies (rice, beans, corn, sugar, salt, cooking oil, and the rare donation of fruit or vegetables), but had to purchase or grow other items. Because they were no longer refugees, the level of external support had declined, and their diet had deteriorated; malnutrition among children was a growing concern. The plan was to gradually shift to a market economy for all goods, including food, with services like health and education provided free. People generally would support themselves through wages and could augment their income by selling produce from family parcels, handicrafts, or other items. Those unable to work—the elderly, the disabled, single women with large families—would be entitled to community support for their basic needs, although the economic logistics of this had not been worked out in detail.

Certain aspects of the communal life-style developed in the refuge had diminished, largely because of competing priorities. There were no longer children's coordinators, for example. With a thousand men and women needed for working in construction, the community simply could not spare adults for this task. Indeed, the organization of the community by sector (i.e., men, women, children, youth, etc.) was temporarily in abeyance, until the first stages of physical development were completed. The introduction of commerce meant the accumulation of plastic wrappings and other trash in public places, but a cleanup campaign had to wait until more pressing needs were addressed.

Also, tortilla making had become more privatized. At first, community-wide collective kitchens were set up, but limited resources meant that each kitchen had to make tortillas for over nine hundred people. The increased burden, added to the taxing nature of the work, made it difficult to recruit workers (typically women). After considerable discussion, the decision was made to prepare tortillas only for people who were working or who otherwise could not make their own (like the elderly). For the rest, mills were set up to grind the corn, so the work was still collectivized to some extent.

Every morning, beginning at around four o'clock, the hum of the generator-powered mills could be heard in each asentimiento. A steady stream of people—usually women and girls but often boys as well—would walk to them carrying containers of washed corn to be ground for the day's tortillas. And at mealtimes, others who were in work structures could be seen carrying small stacks of tortillas, prepared for them in collective kitchens. Throughout the day, the sounds of women's strong hands slapping and palming the

A champa surrounded by the family's milpa, perhaps the central symbol of what it meant to leave the "prison without walls."

The banner says: FMLN and Government: A Sincere Dialogue, A True Peace.

masa joined the shouts of children and the calling of roosters as the background sounds of the community.

Although women now had to individually cook tortillas for their children each morning, many said they didn't mind because the tortillas could be served fresh and hot for each meal. Some people saw this as a step backward for the position of women. Aleida, the responsable for the animal granjas, expressed that concern: "The only thing I see is, it's good in this respect: the people decided that's what they want. It extends the rights of the people to decide. If we [the leadership] said, 'No, it's better the other way,' we'd be taking away the people's right to decide."

▲   ▲   ▲

In some ways, the repatriated refugees were drawn back to a life-style they had left behind, at the same time they were navigating toward a new future. "After being closed in for nine years, people who beforehand had a lot of land around them, the first important thing about being here for them was space and liberty," explained Luis P., head of the community's Urban Development Commission. He was reacting to complaints that the houses being constructed were too small and spaced too close together. These concerns reflected the complexity of transforming people with deep campesino roots into urban dwellers.

"The lots are the standard width of a city lot in El Salvador, ten meters," Luis pointed out. "There is room to expand the houses back into the lot, because it's long. The standard depth of a city lot is twenty meters, but here they're thirty to fifty meters, depending on the size of the family. The

Teaching mathematics in a provisional classroom under the trees.

problem is that people's concept of what a city is like is inaccurate." After all, he continued, "their consciousness as peasants was formed over centuries and centuries. You don't erase that in ten years. No matter how intense the experience was and how much they learned in the refuge, ten years alone doesn't erase generations of experience."

A similar conflict arose when work crews began constructing the new houses. Some objected to returning the tools at the end of the workday so that inventory could be maintained. "Here's the problem," Luis explained. "For a peasant, a tool is the thing he uses to earn his living in a confrontation with the world. If you take away his tools, you take away his life. But that's because a peasant works in an individual way, the peasant and his tool fighting against the world. The fact that it was very difficult for the men to give back the tools was a product of their original consciousness formation as peasants. But this is a collective project, not an individual one. So this was explained to the workers, why there had to be an inventory, why they had to give the tools back."

The evolution of consciousness of these former campesinos and refugees is symbolized by their decision to call their new settlement a city instead of a town or village. "The idea of living together in community came before the idea of a city," explained don Chico, who worked with CODECO. "Before the death of Segundo Montes, we had the idea of coming here and being a community. But the idea of forming a city came later. In the camp, we didn't talk about a city. Not until we came here did we talk about a city." Margarita C., a co-worker, added, "We don't really know what a city is because we always lived in the country. Very few of us had a chance to go to a city. We see it's totally different in every aspect. Life is different, there are more opportunities to improve. In health, there are more opportunities for service. The houses, the streets are fixed up. . . . There are things you have in a city, like parks. We have to have these things here." Don Chico became thoughtful: "One thing we do know is that when cities exist, they had their founders. Here, we're the founder, and the founder gives the idea of what a city will be like."

For *these* founders a city is a place where people live and work together cooperatively, a principle built into the formal structures of Ciudad Segundo Montes—democratic governance, cooperative enterprises, egalitarian resource allocation—but evident in more spontaneous ways. "Some wonderful things are happening," one leader described with pride. "Didn't they tell you in El Barrial about the collective parcel they've developed there? It's

Distributing a donated truckload of potatoes.

Clearing weeds from among the cornrows in the milpa.

a beautiful thing. Every family has gotten a parcel of land, but there are some people who can't work their parcels. For instance, single mothers with a lot of kids, or elderly people who don't have the strength. So they put together the parcels of some of these people, and others in the community set aside time each week to donate work for this parcel." This was not a plan developed by the leadership; it was a grass-roots expression of the deeply ingrained sense of mutuality that developed in the refuge and continues to flourish in Meanguera.

Developing a city also meant an industrial rather than agricultural economic base for the community. The repatriated refugees were skilled workers now, not just farmers; their intention was to develop local industries in the production areas they had learned in Colomoncagua. Northern Morazán, a poor region whose economy had been restricted to growing maguey cactus (for sisal fiber) and coffee and cutting pine lumber, was to become largely self-sufficient; the surrounding population would provide agricultural products, and Ciudad Segundo Montes would produce light industrial goods such as clothing, shoes, tools, and bricks. But all this depended on enough outside assistance to erect factories and purchase start-up materials. And in any event, everything was on hold until the houses in the new city were all completed.

▲   ▲   ▲

The young man with the megaphone moves among the champas announcing a general meeting of the asentimiento of Los Quebrachos. It is five o'clock, and the day's work is over. People gather slowly; within an hour

This retired man went to different kindergarten classes, leading the children in songs and exercises.

The church in the village of San Fernando, its facade destroyed by a 500-pound bomb dropped by a government plane. Before it was damaged, this church could be seen from the refugee camp.

Families bring their cooked, soft corn to be ground in one of the mills, which start operating at 4:00 A.M.

there are perhaps two hundred standing around the rough wooden boards that serve as a stage. The *comunal*, a local elected community official, uses the megaphone to address the crowd.

"Starting a week from today, you have to make a little corral so the pigs and goats don't go out disturbing the neighbors, damaging what they've planted. Or else you have to tie them up. If you don't and the animals cause damage, the owner will have to pay for it. This is to begin a new life. We want to be very clear about this, that within a city animals can't be running about on the streets. . . . We're talking about a city here, a city is being built. So everything has to be based on these rules."

When he asks for comments a woman calls out, "But there's no material for making corrals," and another supports her concern, "There are no ropes for tying up the pigs." The comunal acknowledges the problem: "Yes, we're very limited in materials. Making the corrals is the only reason we accept for cutting branches off the trees, because we don't have anything else to use."

The comunal has other items on his agenda and checks his notes frequently. After each item—preventing children from damaging fruit trees and the growing corn, keeping the latrines clean, and so forth—he solicits reactions from the audience. By now the excited chatter and laughter from the children make it hard to hear him clearly. But people remain patient.

"Okay, so these are the points we have, this is part of building a new kind of life in the city. We're not going to live like we did in the countryside, like we used to live before. It's not the same." He waits for a few moments, looking around to see if anyone wishes to speak. "The community has the floor now to ask questions, or if you have any contributions to make." The meeting has gone on for almost an hour. "If everything is clear now, we'll end. Thank you very much for attending." People go back to their homes, the children's excitement at the event still reverberating in the evening air.

The comunales are elected by voice vote at assemblies in each of the asentimientos. Responsible for communicating decisions made by the citywide leadership bodies to people at the base and for transmitting concerns from the bottom up, they are part of what the community calls "popular democracy." Each colonia elects a coordinator in the same way.

In San Luis, the newly elected comunal calls an assembly, where the main topic is to thank the people for having confidence in him, to pledge his

Laying a flagstone floor in the house that serves as headquarters for the Urban Development Commission.

commitment to the people, and to ask for help in carrying out his duties. After the meeting, he explained the election process: "In the meeting, someone would nominate someone else, and the community would agree by voice. There were five candidates; three of them were women. We each were presented to the community and said something so they knew who we were. Then everyone twenty years old and over could vote. The one with the most votes was chosen—me."

▲   ▲   ▲

In some ways, the community's plans for the new city seemed grandiose, especially considering the primitive state of the physical infrastructure in their settlements in Meanguera, where people lived in huts or shacks with no electricity, running water, or telephones, without paved roads, sewers, or sidewalks. This was especially true considering that their economic situation was roughly comparable—and in some respects, superior—to that of the rest of the population of Morazán. People in the villages may have had a better diet and more substantial houses, but the repatriated refugees brought with them more personal possessions and social resources than existed in the surrounding area. For example, there had been no electric service in the area for nearly a decade; the repatriation meant diesel-powered generators would once again provide electricity to workshops and other common areas.

But the plans for a new city were there, in the architects' and engineers' drawings, in the publications of the community, in the enthusiastic descriptions offered by so many people. "This is not what it's going to be like," María Luisa gestured with her arm at the roughly built comedor where she worked and the champas across the way. "It's going to be something beautiful, our city. This is just the beginning!"

▲   ▲   ▲

The staff of the Urban Development Commission explains how the community's ideas took shape. "What we saw was that [building houses] couldn't be done in an anarchic way—it needed an order, planning. We had to define residential zones, industrial zones, health, education, and so forth. This required a professional urban planning project, which was set up by FASTRAS. They contracted with a group of professional architects to do the planning. This is the result." Huge sheets of architect's blueprints are unrolled and the details are explained. The community's original hexagonal designs have been replaced by more complex plans based on the actual physical terrain of the five asentimientos and the specialized functions they will carry. "This will be the center for government institutions, the post office, ANTEL [the phone company], the municipal government. Delegations of ministries will be here." Another roll of paper is laid out as descriptions and dreams spill forth. "We think that a city can't be complete without

Constructing one of the viviendas mínimas. The wood, nails, and tools had all been brought from Colomoncagua.

recreation and cultural areas. So we'll have schools over here. The idea has slipped out that someday we'll have a university there. . . . This will be a residential area, mostly for teachers. And here there'll be a recreational area—for a zoo and a park, so people can go for a picnic. Maybe we'll put in an artificial lake; the engineers say it will be possible. And we'll have inns or hospitality places for workers and visitors who come here."

The two leaders smile as they admit that they don't understand the technical aspects of the plans. "These professional things, we don't know anything about these. But we've talked to the engineers, and they will begin to teach us, at our level. The engineers are very open to this. . . . We'll train people in architectural and technical drawing and design. Every one of these maps has to be paid for, so if we can do the work ourselves, we'll benefit."

They explain that before work had started, there was discussion in the Asamblea General and throughout the entire community about the plans for the new city. "In the beginning, we did a written survey about the concerns of the community. . . . For example, families of just two or three members were worried that they wouldn't get houses, since there weren't enough materials and priority was given to large families. We made the decision to make larger houses that could be subdivided into two or three households. Another concern was whether they'd be allowed to have animals, and we decided, yes they could."

As they speak, workers are putting in a flagstone floor for the office, made of stones taken from a nearby stream. They want to make this building particularly nice, to show how the new city will work and encourage the community's efforts.

▲   ▲   ▲

Meanwhile, the war in El Salvador was still going on. In government-controlled areas of the country, well-equipped soldiers were everywhere, riding around in tanks and trucks, high-powered weapons always at the ready. These young men, often recruited by gang-pressing youth on the streets of cities and villages, appeared nervous and defensive. Their officers were reluctant to be interviewed and forbade photographs.

North of the Torola River, in one of the areas of the country controlled by the FMLN, the only soldiers to be seen were occasional guerrillas in their more informal dress, carrying AK47s or M16s and lighter packs. So as not to endanger the community, the guerrillas stayed clear of Ciudad Segundo Montes, but could be seen in the other towns in the area. Some were young women, their long hair flowing from beneath olive green caps. A few were older men, with the deeply lined faces of peasants. But most were very young men. These *compas* clearly felt at home and comfortable with the civilian population. Both rank-and-file troops and officers readily engaged visitors in conversation and had no objection to being photographed.

The government had recently stopped bombing civilian areas indiscriminately, so the frequent sounds of helicopters and small planes did not cause panic; most people just glanced up and then continued with their work. Occasional gunfire could be heard, and again, most people acted calmly although they were curious to find out where the fighting was taking place. And sometimes there were real battles close by.

At about half past six one morning, as we left the comedor where we had eaten breakfast, the helicopter we had heard flying around suddenly opened fire with a machine gun almost directly overhead. "There's going to be fighting nearby," said María Luisa as she cleaned up. Shortly after, a small A-37 plane appeared and started circling, looking for a target. Several people stood around watching, although most continued working. After a while, the plane rocketed a hillside, then left. A helicopter flew overhead and fired a couple of rockets, which exploded quite nearby. "That was at the *desvío* (the turnoff) to Jocoaitique," explained one of our neighbors; the explosions were less than two kilometers from where we were standing. Others told us that government soldiers had walked up the road in the middle of the night.

Carrying leather brought from Colomoncagua, which will be used in the shoemaking workshop when it resumes activity.

For the next few hours, we could hear occasional bursts of rifle fire and exploding hand grenades. Then, at about ten o'clock, a new helicoper appeared and landed on the road near the fighting, apparently to evacuate government casualties. A little later the government soldiers started coming down the road in two large groups—over one hundred in all, the size of a company. They walked silently, avoiding contact with bystanders, some averting their faces. People from the community stood on the sides of the road watching the soldiers. Most were silent, although there was some good-natured taunting. As a soldier passed by with a towel over his head, sheltering his face from the hot sun, María Luisa called from the comedor, "What's the matter? Do you have a headache?" When the last soldier walked by, a large group of youngsters ran out and followed him down the road, laughing and calling out, referring to us, "Your pictures are going to turn out nice!" Shortly after, a small group of guerrillas came by, checking to make sure that the soldiers had really left and then fading back into the hills.

The battle was over. (We later learned from interviewing people in Jocoaitique that there had been four to six government casualties, but no guerrilla or civilian injuries. One house had minor damage from a rocket.) The people who had been standing around began to return to their work.

There was a buzz of discussion; everyone was curious about the details of the fighting, but there had been no displays of fear, and in a short time life was back to normal.

This was all according to form. Since the FMLN stayed clear of the community, fighting took place only on its outskirts or in nearby villages. People from Ciudad Segundo Montes were in the most danger during their frequent visits to other places. The guerrillas complained that the army's use of the calle negra as a safe and convenient route violated the neutrality of the settlement and of the new bridge; they had pledged not to attack the bridge as long as it was not militarized.

"Do you see that banner?" asked Chona M., another guide from the Reception Committee, which hosts visitors to the community. A large banner had been erected on one side of the road, calling on the FMLN and the government to engage in sincere negotiations and find a peaceful solution to the conflict. "It used to be across the road. One army patrol tore it down, and we all went and complained to their officer, and he apologized, but we never put it back across the road because we were afraid they'd take it down again."

So the people of Ciudad Segundo Montes were not caught in battles, as other communities were, and they were not experiencing the bombings of civilian targets, which had so devastated the nearby towns. But they felt the war in other ways. Some people were captured by the military as they shopped or visited in a nearby town and were released only after great pressure from the community, often only after being tortured. Vehicles and visitors still had to get permission from the military detachment in Gotera to cross the Torola River. Trucks bringing supplies were often delayed or searched; once a shipment of two hundred books, donated by the Spanish government, was confiscated under the pretext that it included subversive literature. Fuel was particularly difficult to bring into the community because the military assumed it would be used by the FMLN. Self-sufficiency and economic development were made much more difficult by this constant suspicion and frequent harassment.

The community was learning to defend itself against such attacks. The leadership had become skillful at negotiations with government officials, and was treated with more respect by them. Ordinary people had learned how to make their voices heard when someone was being threatened; their experience of living in community gave them confidence and security they had never had before. "Before, we were spread out, but it's better this way," stated a middle-aged woman, still sweating from her job of carrying lumber for the construction of the new houses. "If someone has a problem, if a soldier grabs him, we can go together. If we're all together, if one person has food, we all eat. We take care of each other," she added, smiling broadly.

The people of Ciudad Segundo Montes are no strangers to war and adversity. Throughout their lives they have had to struggle against poverty, repression, and violence. It was only through enormous courage and persistence that they managed to surmount these obstacles and build a new life for themselves, and they are unlikely to be deterred by continued hardships. When peace finally comes to their country—especially if it is a peace based on

Children of the community watch government soldiers as they come down the calle negra after combat with the FMLN.

respect for human rights—they hope to realize the fruits of this long effort so that their children may live in harmony and prosperity.

The coordinator of youth programs in Ciudad Segundo Montes, Caty, a nineteen-year-old who had grown up in the refugee camp, summarized the outlook of her generation, those young people poised to become the community's new leaders: "We lived for ten years in exile. Maybe if we hadn't been there we wouldn't have had these experiences. We learned so much. . . . Most of us were very little when we went into the refuge, and we hadn't yet accepted the values of capitalism, individualism, selfishness; they hadn't yet entered our consciousness." She paused and reflected on the irony of the situation. "We consider that a very favorable condition of our development. If we'd lived longer in [El Salvador], it would have been more difficult to become organized, to think about serving the community. . . . We've come back into a capitalist system, the same one our parents lived in, but we've had the experience of being in an autonomous community, of deciding for ourselves what our values are."

CONCLUSION

▲▲▲▲▲▲▲▲▲▲▲▲▲▲▲▲▲▲▲

CONCLUSION

▲▲

"Why are you writing a book about us now?" one member of the community asked us. "We are just beginning—you ought to wait for a few years." It was July 1990; we had returned to El Salvador for a month to work on the final chapter of this book. In one sense, Juan José was right; things were just getting started there, and the most interesting story was yet to happen. In this sense, our book is about the *pre*history of the community. The real test of their ability to put their ideas, their values, their hopes and dreams into practice in El Salvador will come over the next few years.

But the story of how these extraordinary people came together and created a new life seems important enough that we would want to tell it even if we were less optimistic about the community's future. And understanding why they were able to achieve so much can teach us about the possibilities for democratic development in the area, and perhaps in other parts of the world.

Dr. Segundo Montes identified several reasons for the success of the refugee community in Colomoncagua. Their confinement under conditions of hostility and isolation drew them together and forced them to organize in order to survive. Their homogeneity, especially in shared values and common life experiences, further encouraged cohesiveness. And the assistance they received from international agencies propelled them ahead in skills, understanding, and capability.

We would add two additional factors. First, there was success itself. As the community took steps to protect themselves and improve their situation, they recognized their own capacity for self-direction. Each achievement— organizing to feed themselves and meet their other needs, promoting literacy,

Overleaf: The major work area was construction, which because of its urgency engaged a disproportionately large percentage of the available work force. Here, workers dig gutters at the sides of the roads, an essential precaution during the rainy season.

halting attacks by Honduran soldiers, producing goods in the workshops— led to the confidence that they could go even further, that more fundamental transformation was indeed possible.

The second was the role played by internationals—agency staff and, to a lesser extent, foreign visitors. In addition to providing the community with tangible services and support, these individuals had a subtler and perhaps more profound impact. Before coming to Colomoncagua, the refugees had been provincial in the literal sense of the word. Many, especially women, had scarcely ventured beyond their villages and the immediate surroundings, knowing little of life outside of the campo. But during their nine years in exile, they shared their lives with well-educated people from many parts of the world. At any one time there were up to fifteen agency staff working inside the camp, highly dedicated men and women who often stayed for several years and came to share the refugees' vision. And each month as many as thirty visitors—journalists, researchers, religious and solidarity delegations—came to the camp, and later to Meanguera, to see firsthand this unique community. Through these contacts, the refugees were given a taste of the complexity of the world outside and exposed to a breadth of experience and knowledge inaccessible to most Salvadoran peasants. The questions and observations of visitors encouraged the community to look at themselves as others saw them, fostering a self-consciousness and articulateness usually reserved for those on a more advanced cultural level.

People in the community credit the international volunteers with providing critical support for many of their projects. "When we first came to Colomoncagua, it was clear that there was no organization at all," explained Cristina, a member of the junta directiva in Ciudad Segundo Montes. "The need to organize ourselves was clear. At this point, there were a lot of people coming to help—Hondurans and foreigners. They brought ideas with them, and people took hold of those ideas."

Similarly, Caty described the key input from internationals in the community's attempts to build an organization for youth in the refuge. "It was hard for us at first because we never had any experience in organizing, nothing like a youth club or anything. But we had help from international visitors. They helped us organize." With this support, the refugees set up a youth center in Colomoncagua, offering a variety of recreational and social activities. Caty and her fellow youth coordinators looked forward to the arrival in Meanguera of a Belgian who would help them secure funds to reactivate youth activities there.

As the community became more confident and clear about their goals, their relationship with internationals moved from dependency to collaboration. Speaking of the contributions of agency personnel who continued to work for them even after repatriation, Cristina pointed out, "The more we advance, the more we need people who've been trained, not just technically, but who've developed the consciousness of the need to support the community, so the project of the community can go forward and not collapse."

Finally, there is the more complex and politically sensitive issue of the role played by organizers from religious groups, popular organizations, and even FMLN-aligned parties in El Salvador, who provided leadership and direction for the refugees. The community was always under suspicion of being a den of guerrillas and was subject to attacks on the basis of this accusation. "Ever since we were in Colomoncagua, there were some who accused us of being guerrillas or communists," said Mercedes C., from the Reception Committee. "Our answer was, we were refugees. If we were guerrillas, we'd have been here [in El Salvador], not there. And we're a community of women, children, old people." But the political situation in El Salvador (and Honduras) is such that the communal, egalitarian values espoused by the people of Colomoncagua made them vulnerable to charges of subversion, and repression made it dangerous to admit to any outside influences.

Because of the obvious dangers from being in any way linked to the FMLN, it was difficult for the role of organizers to be openly acknowledged. For this reason, we are unable to assess the extent to which leadership in the community came from these outside forces as opposed to being entirely organic and indigenous. Similarly, we are unable to credit organizations for genuine contributions they may have made to the development of the community. Undoubtedly, this part of the story will be told only when the situation in El Salvador has changed dramatically, when groups and individuals advocating social justice are no longer seen as a threat to the established order.

The community acknowledged that many people came to Colomoncagua and Meanguera to help them, including some from radical political organizations. "If someone comes, no matter from where, if it's clear that they have the interests of the community at heart, they'll be listened to," explained one of the top leaders. "People who have better ideological development can say, 'This has worked in some places.' They can give suggestions that have better results. We're an open community here that has learned a new way to think. Now if someone comes, no matter from where, they can talk with us. If we like what they say, okay." He went on, "We're peasants, what do we know? So if someone comes to help us . . . we'll take advantage of their offer, no matter what their politics."

"You have to remember that we are Salvadorans," one of the women pointed out. "Like any community in this country, some of us have relatives who are guerrillas, and others have relatives who are in the military. And some people are not connected to either armed band."

What is clear is that no organizers who tried to move the community in a direction it was unwilling to go would have had any success. The strong emphasis on participation and openness, on consensus and voluntarism, as well as the highly democratic structures and procedures established in the community would have thwarted any efforts to control the community from outside or from within. Occasionally one would meet a leader or a rank-and-file member of the community who was more educated than the rest or

The main traffic on the road is pedestrian. With the return of the refugees, the other residents of the area felt it was safe to use the calle negra once more.

exhibited a political style that was more advanced. But the ability of these individuals to function as leaders was still contingent on their winning support through their effectiveness and dedication. Thus, while sympathetic organizations may have provided leadership that functioned in cooperation with indigenous leaders, no one was simply directing things from the outside, as the simplistic denunciations by the Honduran, Salvadoran, and United States authorities claimed.

Leaders were sensitive to the need of staying in touch with the grass roots. For example, a member of the team in charge of urban development in Ciudad Segundo Montes explained why they had asked an international development agency for a motorcycle. "It's so that we can ride around easily but still be in touch with people," he said. If you don't maintain contact with the community, he went on, there will be serious problems. "First, you get lost in your own vision, and the people at the base get lost in *your* vision. Second, people will lose confidence in you and your ability to make decisions. This is all about building a framework of dialogue within which the process of development can take place."

The community's philosophy of *auto-gestión* (self-management), nourished since the early days in Colomoncagua, shapes their relationship to outsiders. Just as they had insisted in the camp that international agencies not administer their programs, but train refugees (perhaps the key source of the earlier conflict with MSF), so they made similar demands on government and humanitarian agencies in El Salvador. When they appealed to the Ministry of Public Health for assistance in maintaining their program of vaccinations for children, for example, the community insisted that they administer the campaign themselves and that the government provide vaccines, syringes, and other supplies. And a British humanitarian agency that sent a delegation to consider financing the brick factory and other enterprises learned that the project would be accepted only on condition that the community itself, and not the agency, actually administer the program.

▲   ▲   ▲

Just what is the community's vision of their future? They want a society in which people act in mutual support and consideration to achieve a level of economic, cultural, and social development not possible under traditional Salvadoran arrangements. Neither exploitation nor authoritarianism in the name of progress is acceptable to them. They saw in Colomoncagua that people can live this way, and now they are testing their ability to create their new life without either the restrictions or the protections of the refugee camp.

In the economic arena, they are encouraging private initiative from individual members and involvement by businesspeople from outside the community to coexist with production and distribution cooperatives and collectively owned enterprises and resources. Politically, they are constructing an open local democracy, responsive to grass-roots initiative. Their approach clearly would not fit into orthodox communist or socialist schemes. Flexibility in confronting problems and unforeseen developments is highly valued, and political or ideological rhetoric is rarely encountered in their conversations, publications, or documents. In fact, one way to dismiss a political position in the community is to describe it as "schematic" or "rigid."

Some people may see an influence in the collapse of Stalinist regimes in Eastern Europe here, and we would not deny some effect. More to the point is the history of the Salvadoran revolutionary and popular movements in general. Over the period from the late 1970s to the late 1980s, those movements—responding to their own experiences of organization and repression—moved from traditional leftist rhetoric to a more pragmatic acceptance of economic and political pluralism, and a desire for political engagement and negotiations. Positions that did not correspond to political and historical reality were described as too "ideological" or "radical." In this context, the open, flexible posture the community consciously and proudly adopts should be seen not so much as a reaction to the immediate

Attending a grass-roots meeting.

events of 1989–1990, but as the outcome of a decade or more of experience, both in El Salvador as a whole and in Colomoncagua and Meanguera.

Also, Ciudad Segundo Montes is not functioning in isolation. The community works with PADECOMSM on the development of the entire zone and with FASTRAS, a nationwide confederation of communities and co-operatives. Their repatriation was not unique; the entire camp at San Antonio and most of the refugees in Mesa Grande have also returned and are establishing similar communities in different rural zones, though perhaps none with such an ambitious project.

Finally, the success of this community will in the end depend not only on their commitment and skill, but also on the greater Salvadoran context. Although by fall of 1990 there had not been serious repression from the military, continual negotiations with the authorities were necessary in order to carry out very basic activities. In the short time we were there, it became increasingly difficult for visitors to get permission to enter the community, because the local colonel tightened control, insisting on safe-conduct passes from the armed forces high command, valid only for three-day visits. The community is well aware that the repression repatriated villages in Chaletenango have experienced—including the rocketing of houses in the settlement of Corral de Piedra, resulting in several deaths—could be turned against them as well.

The main weapons the community has to confront the uncertainties and dangers before them are the experiences in the camp, their commitment to their own project, and the support of individuals and organizations both in El Salvador and internationally. They represent a model for other rural communities in Central America of development based on a conscious, collective decision to create a new identity, to determine their own course, and to construct their own future—not in splendid isolation, but in relations of mutual support with other peoples and communities.

▲   ▲   ▲

As night falls in Meanguera, the people of Ciudad Segundo Montes gather around their fires, taking care of last-minute chores and getting the children settled for the night. Quiet sounds of conversation, laughter, and singing mingle with radio broadcasts of music and news and the chriping of night insects and frogs. The smell of wood smoke fills the air. The sky is very broad and very dark; in the far distance lightning illuminates the mountains. Even for those whose homes are set farther apart, the sense that others are nearby is strong.

Circumstance brought these people together and thrust them into their special historical role. Had war not uprooted them, they would undoubtedly have lived out their lives as campesinos, working the land to feed themselves and their children. Their journey from that starting point was filled with tragedy and loss; if they could, many would probably choose to go back in time and undo the events of the past decade. But they were never given such a choice, and so they faced each sorrow and hardship with determination to persevere, to overcome. The sorrows and hardships were slowly replaced by accomplishments and joy.

Now they are moving into a future that they have consciously fashioned out of their experiences and desires. To the extent that they succeed, they will certainly become, as their own motto puts it, "a hope which is being born in the East for all of El Salvador."

ORGANIZATIONAL CHARTS

▲▲

Governance Structure in Colomoncagua, 1988-1989

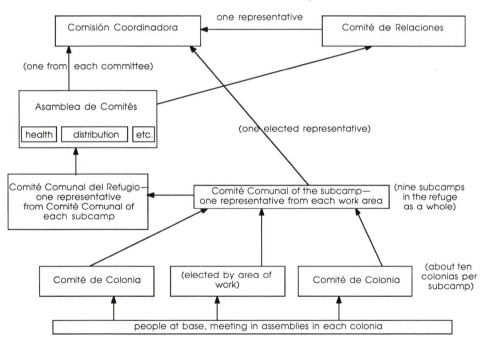

Governance Structure of Ciudad Segundo Montes, July 1990

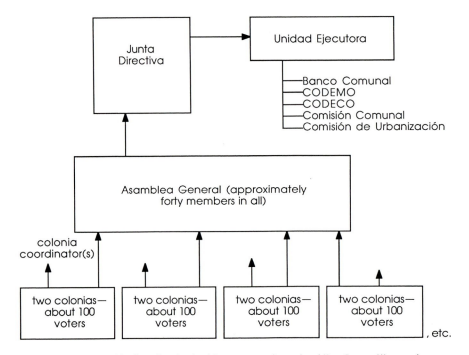

Also, one comunal is directly elected to represent each of the five settlements

A P P E N D I X ▲ B

ORGANIZATIONS WORKING WITH THE NEW COMMUNITY

▲▲

The organization that represents the community of Ciudad Segundo Montes in the United States is:
  Voices on the Border
  P.O. Box 53081
  Temple Heights Station
  Washington, D.C. 20009

In Canada, the address is:
  People for PADECOES
  35 Juliet Crescent
  Toronto, Ontario
  M6M 1N5

In Europe, the community is represented by:
  PROCARES
  Rue de la Tulipe 34
  1050 Bruxelles
  Belgium

The community has an office in San Salvador. Their address for mail is:
  CCSM
  A.P. 3357
  Centro de Gobierno
  San Salvador
  El Salvador

GLOSSARY OF ACRONYMS AND SPANISH WORDS

▲▲▲

Acronyms

ANTEL	The Salvadoran national telecommunications authority
BANCOMO	Communal Bank of Morazán
CEBES	Christian Base Communities of El Salvador
CEDEN	Evangelical Committee for Development and the National Emergency (Honduras)
CIREFCA	International Conference on Central American Refugees (Guatemala, March 1989); it was reconvened in New York during June 1990
CODECO	Committee for Commercial Development (Meanguera)
CODEMO	Committee for Development and Emergency in Morazán
CONARE	National Commission on Refugees (Honduran government agency)
CRS	Catholic Relief Services
FASTRAS	Salvadoran Foundation for Workers' Self-Management and Solidarity
FMLN	Farabundo Martí Front for National Liberation (El Salvador)
IDHUCA	Human Rights Institute of the Central American University (San Salvador)
MSF	Médecins Sans Frontières (Doctors Without Borders)
PADECOES	Council for Community Development of El Salvador
PADECOMSM	Council for Community Development of Morazán and San Miguel
UNHCR	United Nations High Commission for Refugees (often referred to by its Spanish acronym, ACNUR)

Spanish Words

almacén	warehouse for distribution
asamblea	assembly
asentimiento	settlement
atol	a sweet drink made from corn
auto-gestión	self-management
bienvenida	welcome
bodega	warehouse for storage
calle	street, row, road
campesino(a)	peasant, country person, farm worker
campo	countryside; also used in El Salvador for a soccer field
cantón	township (in El Salvador)
capacitación	training, developing skills
carpa	tent
carpintería	carpentry
casería	small rural population center—smaller than what we would call a village
champa	hut
charamusca	an ice made from fruit juices and frozen in a small plastic bag
charla	talk, presentation
cipote	kid, youngster (Central American slang)
ciudad	city
colonia	neighborhood
colón, colones	Salvadoran currency
comal	flat metal or clay cooking surface, like a skillet, used in Mexico and Central America to cook tortillas
comedor	diner; a modest eatery
comisión	commission
comité	committee
compañero(a)	partner, comrade, companion, mate
compa	diminutive of compañero used to refer to guerrillas, who are also sometimes called *los muchachos,* the boys or the kids
comunal	communal, collective; also used in Ciudad Segundo Montes as the title of someone in charge of a communal area—e.g., the *comunal* of an *asentimiento.*
conjunto	group, musical band
coordinador(a)	coordinator, coordinating
costura	sewing
cuartel	barracks; military headquarters
cuma	a large knife, generally curved but sometimes straight, used extensively in agricultural work. The *cuma* is the basic tool of the *campesino.*
despedida	farewell
desvío	detour; turnoff from a main road

don, doña	honorific title, somewhat formal, used with the first name of the person addressed (don José, doña María)
fábrica	factory
fresco	fruit drink (in El Salvador)
granja	barn, animal-raising project
guardería	nursery, day-care center
herrería	ironworking, hardware, smithy
hojatalería	tinsmithing
hola!	hi!
hortaliza	vegetable; used to indicate a vegetable garden
jarcia	cords, weaving done with cords
kinder	preschool, kindergarten
manualidad	manual skills
masa	dough, corn dough
mecánica	mechanics
milpa	cornfield (in Mexico and Central America)
norte	north, the north wind
noticiero	news program or newsletter
pila	battery, cement sink with water storage
pipián	a type of summer squash
quebrada	ravine
refugiado	refugee
refugio	refuge
relación	relation
repatriado	repatriated person
responsable	person in charge
retén	checkpoint
salvador	savior
sobador(a)	folk masseur
tamal	a sort of boiled corn cake, made of corn dough wrapped in banana leaves for cooking. They are stuffed in a variety of ways. One recipe, popular on weekends and at Christmas, is called *nacatamal*.
telenovela	soap opera
tranca	gate or sliding post to lock doors; a military checkpoint with a barrier across the road
vivienda	dwelling
vos	you. Informal personal pronoun used instead of *tú* in much of Central America and some other countries.
zapato	shoe
zopilote	buzzard (Central American usage)

SUGGESTED READINGS

▲▲

General Introductions

For readers who are interested in getting a good overview of what has been going on in Central America, we recommend the following books: Tom Barry, Beth Wood, and Deb Preusch, *Dollars and Dictators: A Guide to Central America* (Albuquerque: The Resource Center, 1982); Walter LeFeber, *Inevitable Revolutions: The United States in Central America* (New York: Norton, 1983); Jenny Pearce, *Under the Eagle: U.S. Intervention in Central America and the Caribbean* (Boston: South End Press, 1982).

To follow developments in Latin America, of the many good publications currently available, we find the following to be among the most useful: *NACLA Report on the Americas*, 475 Riverside Drive, #454, New York, NY 10115; *Nation*, 72 Fifth Avenue, New York, NY 10011; *Inter-Hemispheric Education Resource Center*, Box 4506, Albuquerque, NM 87196

El Salvador

The following books provide an introduction to the situation in El Salvador and the history of the refugees: Robert Armstrong and Janet Shenk, *El Salvador: The Face of Revolution* (Boston: South End Press, 1982); Tom Barry, *El Salvador: A Country Guide* (Albuquerque: The Resource Center, 1990); Phillip Berryman, *Liberation Theology* (New York: Pantheon, 1987); Berryman's *The Religious Roots of Rebellion: Christians in Central American Revolutions* (Maryknoll, N.Y.: Orbis Books, 1984); Raymond Bonner, *Weakness and Deceit* (New York: Times Books, 1984); Renato Camarda, *Forced to Move* (San Francisco: Solidarity Publications, 1985); Charles Clements, *Witness to War* (New York: Bantam, 1984); Yvonne Dilling, *In Search of Refuge* (Scottdale, Pa.: Herald Press, 1984); Lawyers Committee for International Human Rights, *El Salvador's Other Victims: The War on the Displaced* (New York: Lawyers Committee for International Human Rights and Americas Watch, 1984); Lawyers Committee for International Human Rights, eds., *Honduras: A Crisis on the Border* (New York: Lawyers Committee for International Human Rights, 1985); Penny Lernoux, *People of God: The Struggle for World Catholicism* (New

York: Viking, 1989); Tommie Sue Montgomery, *Revolution in El Salvador* (Boulder, Colo.: Westview, 1982); Jack Nelson-Pallmeyer, *War against the Poor: Low-Intensity Conflict and Christian Faith* (Maryknoll, N.Y.: Orbis Books, 1989); New Americas Press, eds., *A Dream Compels Us: Voices of Salvadoran Women* (Boston: South End Press, 1989); Marilyn Thomson, *Women of El Salvador: The Price of Freedom* (Philadelphia: Institute for the Study of Human Issues, 1986); Scott Wright, Minor Sinclair, Margaret Lyle, and David Scott, eds., *El Salvador: A Spring Whose Waters Never Run Dry* (Washington, D.C.: Ecumenical Program on Central America and the Caribbean [EPICA], 1990).